Praise for *Zombie Spaceship Wasteland*

"Patton Oswalt . . . is one of those rare performers whose material translates into any medium without losing its sharpness—including, for the first time, print. . . . It is well worth it to join him on his odyssey."

—*The Washington Post*

"A believable portrait of a witty, vulnerable funnyman. The autobiographical passages . . . have the detail and emotional nuance of fine short stories."

—*Entertainment Weekly*

"[Oswalt] brings that postmodern sensibility to his debut book, a wildly diverse collection of essays that careens from sincere introspection to inventive comedic material that would fit seamlessly into one of his sets. . . . The humor comes from his sharp storytelling and sardonic wit. . . . [Oswalt] populates these stories with expertly drawn characters, and infuses them with a limitless supply of cultural references and deft turns of phrase."

—*The Boston Globe*

"A thoughtful, hilarious, quasi-memoir that puts the standard-issue comedy-routine-in-book-form to shame."

—*SPIN*

"The book echoes Steve Martin's memoir, *Born Standing Up*. . . . Oswalt is trying to convey his own path into comedy without navel-gazing or falling back on tropes."

—*Los Angeles Times*

"[Oswalt] proves he can pen a compellingly entertaining fast read."

—*Fort Worth Star-Telegram*

"Hilarious."

—*Lincoln Journal Star*

"[Oswalt] brings insight and passion to his subjects that lift the book above hipster snark to the level of something you'll want to reread and savor. . . . He also shines a light on a side of Los Angeles that you don't often see or hear about, but that you'll want to visit after devouring this hilarious, incisive read."

—*Penthouse*

"To delve into this book is to take a tour of Oswalt's delightfully offbeat mind. . . . Oswalt is a wonderfully descriptive writer."

—*Booklist*

"Funny and occasionally heartbreaking . . . a cerebral and somewhat surreal tour through the thought processes of Patton Oswalt. It is an inspired and unique work, operating well outside the realm of the disposable comedy memoir."

—*AintItCool.com*

"*Zombie Spaceship Wasteland* is very much a memoir—and a subtly haunting one at that. . . . Thoughtful, poignant prose evoke an aura of loss that permeates the entire collection."

—Splitsider.com

"Alternately revealing, hilarious, and livid, a description that would seem to apply equally to [Oswalt's] work as a stand-up comedian."

—Hitfix.com

"Further proof that Patton Oswalt is way funnier than I am, which is either high praise or an insult. Your call."

—Judd Apatow

"Patton Oswalt is a brilliant rarity: a relentlessly creative and original comic who is also a superb writer. If you don't buy this book you are a fool and I will, I swear, fight you."

—Conan O'Brien

"Funny, thoughtful stuff. Patton alternates the spit-take hilarity of a great stand-up with the quiet, mordant insight that clearly helped make him one. Which is amazing, 'cause he's an idiot."

—Joss Whedon

"Fans of Patton Oswalt's stand-up comedy have always known he was a born writer at heart, and now here's the proof. This is a surprisingly affecting, sincere, and I daresay, vulnerable collection of essays, all keenly observed, always very funny."

—Dave Eggers

"I don't know what's sharper, Oswalt's brains or Oswalt's tongue."

—Sarah Vowell

"I have impeccable taste, and I only converse with the following three: God, the Devil, and Patton Oswalt. All three have opened for me. This book is a funny tragedy. You'll laugh, you'll cry, you'll convert to Pattonism. If you do not love this book, remember, I know where you live in your mother's basement."

—Harlan Ellison

"Perfect—I can describe Patton's book the same way I describe his stand-up—brilliant and prolific. I am slack-jawed, amazed, and left feeling both inspired and fraudulent."

—Sarah Silverman

"Patton Oswalt is among the funniest onstage talking humans I am aware of, so it annoys me deeply that he is also an incredibly talented writer. It annoys me, but it does not surprise me. Every sentence in this book is funny (except for the sad ones), but it also brims with Oswaltian smarts and surprising poignancy."

—John Hodgman

ALSO BY
PATTON OSWALT

NOVELS

The Brannock Doom, Devil's Brain-Collector Series

The Forgotten Tomb of the Worm-Serpent
The Remembered Citadel of Screeching Victory
The Lost Mage-Pit
The Discovered Witch-Keep
The Falsely Recovered Troll-Bog Memory

The Thane Star-Mind Series

The Nothing Ray
Song of the Cyrus-5 Dream Hunters
Sand-Riders of the Fifth Sigil
Andro-Borg-Bot
Solar Star
Galactic Universe

CHILDREN'S BOOKS

The Candy Van
A Ewe Named Udo Who Does Judo and Other Poems
Everyone Resents

ZOMBIE
SPACESHIP
WASTELAND

A Book by

Patton Oswalt

SCRIBNER

New York   London   Toronto   Sydney   New Delhi

SCRIBNER
A Division of Simon & Schuster, Inc.
1230 Avenue of the Americas
New York, NY 10020

Certain names and identifying characteristics have been changed,
certain characters are composites, and some are made-up altogether.

First Scribner trade paperback edition November 2011

SCRIBNER and design are registered trademarks of The Gale Group, Inc.,
used under license by Simon & Schuster, Inc., the publisher of this work.

For information about special discounts for bulk purchases,
please contact Simon & Schuster Special Sales at 1-866-506-1949
or business@simonandschuster.com.

The Simon & Schuster Speakers Bureau can bring authors
to your live event. For more information or to book an event
contact the Simon & Schuster Speakers Bureau at 1-866-248-3049
or visit our website at www.simonspeakers.com.

DESIGNED BY ERICH HOBBING

Manufactured in the United States of America

1   3   5   7   9   10   8   6   4   2

Library of Congress Control Number: 2010025144

ISBN 978-1-4391-4908-9
ISBN 978-1-4391-4909-6 (pbk)
ISBN 978-1-4391-5627-8 (ebook)

Credits can be found on p. 265.

For Alice and Michelle

my spaceships away

from the zombie wasteland

She cries black tears!

—Cindy Brady, *The Brady Bunch*

"We're trying to survive a nuclear war here!"
"Yes, but we can do it in style . . ."

—Howard and Marion Cunningham, *Happy Days*

There's nothing in the dark that isn't there in the light.

—Major Frank Burns, *M*A*S*H*

Contents

ZOMBIE
SPACESHIP
WASTELAND

Preface Foreword Intro

In middle school, I started *reading*.

I'd been "reading" since kindergarten. It was dutiful and orderly. Point B followed Point A.

But something happened in middle school—a perfect alignment of parental support and benign neglect. The parental "support" came from keeping me stocked in Beverly Cleary, John Bellairs, *The Great Brain* books, and Daniel Pinkwater. Also *Bridge to Terabithia, The Pushcart War, How to Eat Fried Worms*—and the parallel-universe, one-two mind-crack of *The Bully of Barkham Street* and *A Dog on Barkham Street*.

And then there was the blessed, benign neglect.

The "neglect" grew out of the same "support." My mom and dad were both busy, working jobs and trying to raise two kids during uncertain times. In the rush of trying to find something new for me to read, they'd grab something off the shelf at Waldenbooks after only glancing at the copy on the back.

Whoever did a lousy job writing copy for books like Richard Brautigan's *The Hawkline Monster*, H. P. Lovecraft's *At the Mountains of Madness*, Harlan Ellison's *The*

1

Beast That Shouted Love at the Heart of the World, and Anthony Burgess's *A Clockwork Orange* ("It's about a teenager in the future!" said my mom)—thank you. Thank you thank you *thank you.* You gave me some tangy, roiling stew under the golden crust of the Young Adult literature I was gobbling up.

So yes, I still love Bellairs's *The House with a Clock in Its Walls,* but I always imagine the two bounty killers from *The Hawkline Monster* in its basement, armed for bear and fucking the Magic Child on a rug. And somewhere beyond John Christopher's White Mountains are Vic and Blood, hunting for canned food and pussy. And who prowled the outer woods of Terabithia? Yog-Sothoth, that's who.

It's a gift and an affliction at the same time—constantly wondering how the mundane world I'm living in (or reading about) links to the darker impulses I'm having (or imagining I have). The gift-affliction followed me (or was it guiding me?) through my teens, in 1980s suburban Virginia. The local TV station still showed *The Wolfman* on Saturday mornings—but I'd already read Gary Brandner's *The Howling.* So I couldn't watch Lon Chaney, Jr., lurch around the Scottish countryside without wondering if he craved sex as much as murder. I would recontextualize lines of sitcom dialogue to suit darker needs, the way the Surrealists would obsess over a single title card— "When he crossed the bridge, the shadows came out to meet him"—in the 1922 silent movie *Nosferatu.**

* *Nosferatu* looms over and lurks under everything I'm writing about here, and in this book.

I was five years old and living in Tustin Meadows, California—a point

Then the local TV station gave way to the early years of cable TV. My parents' working hours were such that it was impossible to police my viewing habits. Scooby-Doo and his friends unmasked the Sea Demon and found bitter Old Man Trevers, trying to scare people away from his harbor. But they missed, under the dock, the Humanoids from the Deep, raping sunbathers. Did Harriet the Spy and the Boy Who Could Make Himself Disappear run afoul of Abel Ferrara's Ms. 45, Paul Kersey from *Death Wish*, or the Baseball Furies from Walter Hill's *The Warriors*? *The Pushcart War* took place on the same New York streets where Travis Bickle piloted his taxi. And it sure was cool how the Great Brain could swindle Parley Benson out of his repeating air rifle by pretending to make a magnetic stick. You know what was better? Knowing that, one state over, the bloody slaughter of

---

on the arc of my dad's military career postings, tracing a backward word balloon over the United States, starting in Virginia, up through Ohio, out to California, and back to Virginia.

It was Halloween, and the local library had one of those "kids' activity days," where we made cookies and cut out jack-o'-lanterns and heard ghost stories. And one of the librarians—with nothing but good intentions, I'm sure—decided to show an 8 mm print of *Nosferatu* against a wall. They blacked out the curtains and the projector clattered to life and spit out what I'm sure the adults thought would be a harmless, old spook show.

That movie—F. W. Murnau's *Nosferatu*—burst and spread out and filled that little room with jagged, discordant fever-mares from across continents and decades. The scariest vampire any of us had seen up to that point was the Count on *Sesame Street*. We were screaming and balling our fists up to our chests and wondering how we'd gone from cookies and crafts to a wrinkly rat-man spreading contagion across an already-blasted landscape like a plague that kills plagues. No one in that room ever escaped Max Schreck's curly, cursed talons. Least of all me. I saw how that flat square of sepia light replaced the hard dimensions around us. I wanted to get on the other side of it.

Heaven's Gate was swallowing up John Hurt and Christopher Walken.

Maybe that makes my generation unique—the one that remembers *before* MTV and after . . . and then *before* the Internet and after. The generation I see solidifying itself now? They were *born* connected—plopped out into the late nineties, into the land of Everything That Ever Was Is Available from Now On. What crass acronym will we slap on the thumb-sore texting multitudes of the twenty-first century? The Waifnos? The Wireds? Anything's better than "Gen X," which is what we got. Thanks, Douglas Coupland. We sound like a team of mutant vigilantes with frosted hair and chain wallets. Actually, that's not completely horrible.

And neither was being "Gen X." We'll always cherish the stark, before-and-after culture shift of our adolescence. We had isolation . . . and then access. Drought and then deluge. Three channels and then fifty. CBs and then chat rooms. And our parents didn't have time, in the beginning, to sift through the "Where is all of this new stimulus coming from?" and decide what was beyond our emotional grasp. Thus, the mishmash. Six-color cartoons, but with an edge of gray and maroon. YA literature laced with sex and violence. A generation gifted with confusion, unease, and then revelation.

Not anymore, I guess. It seems that every TV show, movie, song, and website for the generation following me involves protagonists who've been fucking, killing, and cracking wise about fucking and killing since *before* anyone even showed up to watch them. I'm sure that will yield some bizarre new films, books, and music—stuff I can't even imagine. Doesn't matter. By the time that comes around, I'll have long had my consciousness downloaded into a hovering Wolf Husbandry Bot. I'll glide over the Russian steppes, playing Roxy Music's *Avalon,* setting the mood for a lusty canine rutting. I don't care how high my shrink increases my Lexapro dosage—I WANT TO BE A ROBOT THAT HELPS WOLVES HAVE SEX. Otherwise, my parents threw away the money they spent on my college education.

So thank you, Mom and Dad. Thank you, League of Lazy Copywriters. Thank you, reader, for buying this book. I apologize ahead of time for not even trying to aim at Point B, or even starting from Point A. Comedy and terror and autobiography and comics and literature— they're all the same thing.

To me.

FULL DISCLOSURE

Stuff I did on the Internet while writing this introduction:

➤ Looked up the lyrics to Toto's song "99"

➤ Played two "Armor" battles of Gemcraft Chapter 0

➤ Checked the Facebook status of two people I hate

➤ Technorati'd myself

Ticket Booth

I fell asleep and read
Just about every paragraph
—R.E.M., "Feeling Gravitys Pull"

I still dream about them. The three screens and the ticket booth.

I spent my high school years twenty minutes from Washington, DC, in a suburb called Sterling, Virginia. Actually, in a sub-suburb of Sterling called Sugarland Run. But our mailing address was "Sterling." We were, postage-wise, suburban feudal subjects.

And no, we're not going *back* to high school here, to reminisce, balance ledger sheets, or admit failings. I know that high school is the central American experience,* but my memories of what I did in high school are drowned out by what I *missed*. And I missed it by *twenty minutes*.

Twenty minutes from Washington, DC, was twenty minutes from eternal hipster cred—"Oh, I was at that

*At least, that's what Kurt Vonnegut said. Go with your 'gut, always.

7

Fugazi show when I was *fif*teen . . ." "Yeah, well, I stole my parents' credit card and caught Bad Brains at WUST Hall . . ." "The Minor Threat bassist punched me outside of Piccolo's in Georgetown on my birthday . . ."

To give you an idea of how wide a mark I missed this explosive time by, I had to look up most of those bands on Wikipedia. I had no car. I had no money. There was one bus in and out of Sugarland Run, and it stopped running at seven P.M. All the older kids who could've given me a ride into DC had just discovered the Doors, whippets, and doing whippets in their garage while listening to the Doors. My throat still feels floaty and burned whenever I hear "The Crystal Ship." "Strange Days" still tastes like cheap beer in someone's town house when their parents were vacationing.

There was also a plague of divorces among my friends and acquaintances when I was in high school—fallout from the suburban swinging that finally reached Sterling as the seventies were flickering away. We were too young, too gobsmacked by *Star Wars* and *Saturday Night Live* and snow forts and thunderstorms to notice the dalliances that led to the rifts. But we wasted no time taking advantage of the suddenly empty houses on the weekends. And now, one floor below the heartbroken half of a shattered marriage brooding in an upstairs bedroom, we were free to bray along with Zeppelin or the Who or whatever decades-old band we believed we were discovering. I know a lot of people associate the eighties with MTV, post-punk, New Wave, and the second birth of hip-hop, but not us suburban kids. We were broke-ass white boys, plundering our parents' LPs from when they were young and horny. The bands we followed were the ones savvy enough to survive suddenly being filmed—thus, Springsteen pumped iron, Genesis got teddy-bear cute, and Aerosmith hooked up with the cool new black kids. REO Speedwagon, Styx, and Grand Funk Railroad were not so lucky. Zeppelin, the Stones, the Doors, and the Who were safe in their aeries. The importance of adaptation and luck were the first things I learned about music.

But not creation. I wasn't there for it. No one will ever spot my dopey face in a crowd shot from a coffee-table book about the DC hardcore scene. There will be no fleeting glimpses of my underage self in the inevitable documentary about Fugazi. Now that I think of it, I'm sure there *is* a documentary about Fugazi. I know I'm not in it. Maybe my initials are still in the "high score" top 5 on the Galaga machine at Dominion Skating Rink. Someone tell Ken Burns.

I did manage to see Genesis twice on their Invisible Touch tour. The second time I saw them, opening act Paul Young knocked himself unconscious twirling his mike stand around, singing "Everytime You Go Away." No one in the stadium seemed to notice. The lines at the pretzel stands were hella long.

I was trapped, stuck in the syrup of the suburbs. And there, among houses built one year *after* I was born (I had more history than the streets I wandered), I found an underground scene.

Literally, underground.

Subterranean but unheralded. Gone forever and

unmourned. Pungent and vibrant but unchronicled. No one involved brags about it. None of us will be portrayed by Kevin Corrigan, Peter Sarsgaard, or Chloë Sevigny in a brilliant indie biopic about the movers and shakers of said scene.

The Towncenter 3 Movie Theater, in the Sterling Towncenter Shopping Mall of Sterling, Virginia. Right at the intersection of Route 7 and Dranesville Road.

That was my Lapin Agile. My Factory. My Elaine's. My CBGB. My Studio 54.

Most of those places are gone.* So is the Towncenter 3. I think. Sort of. Until recently, it still existed as a movie theater, under the clubfooted name of the Sterling Cinema Drafthouse and the Hollywood Café, Cinema 3 Niteclub. Now their website says, simply, *The Sterling Cinema Draft is closed forever!*

Not to me. Never. And in my mind, it will always be, simply, the Towncenter 3. Three screens. Five employees. One manager. At least, as long as I was there.

I got a job as an usher there in the summer of 1987. You entered at street level, in between a karate studio and a pizza joint. But, due to some weird, Escher-like construction I still don't understand, you *descended* three flights of stairs into a murky, fluorescent-lit lobby and snack area that looked like it should have been in a Nik Ker-

---

*The Lapin Agile and Elaine's, as of this writing, are still going strong. The Factory—and the building that held it—gone. CBGB is a John Varvatos store. Studio 54 is now a theater, with "franchises" all over the world, including a location dropped inside the MGM Grand in Vegas like a core sample of the seventies dropped into a museum of glittery loss.

shaw video. Then, once you bought snacks and drinks, you descended *another* flight of stairs to an even dimmer, grimmer lobby where you'd choose one of three theaters. It was a theater designed like an artless logic problem— which door leads to freedom, which to death, and which to *Adventures in Babysitting*?

The day I was hired was the last day they were showing *RoboCop*. After that, we showed a procession of unanswerable trivia questions like *Jaws: The Revenge*, *Who's That Girl?*, *The Living Daylights*, and *Summer School*.

I'd had some really good times in the Towncenter 3 when I went there as a teen. *Return of the Living Dead*, *Beverly Hills Cop*, and *Richard Pryor: Here and Now*. Now that I could watch anything I wanted, they showed nothing I wanted to see. My fellow employees felt the same way. We were rats locked in a lightless underground warren, toiling under bright, loud distractions beamed onto soda-splattered screens. Now we found ourselves facing a summer where the distractions weren't distracting. Our fancies slowly turned to the . . . unfanciful.

This growing discontent was overseen by Dan the Manager.*

Dan claimed he was an ex–Texas Ranger. Do the Texas Rangers make their members drink a quart of Vladimir vodka every day? If so, Dan was keeping their frontier spirit alive. His face was scorched craggy by fermented

---

*I'm changing everyone's name in this, and some other things. But if any of the people I worked with at the Towncenter 3 are still alive and continued making the choices they made when we drew paychecks together, then they're beyond consequence or remorse and will kill me.

potatoes and not the punishing Laredo sun. He had a swaggering, bowlegged walk that came from personally insulting, every waking second, gravity and inertia—not from sitting astride a noble steed on the prairie. His ten-gallon hat hid his bald, psoriasis-ravaged skull dome.

Cheap liquor is a magic potion than can turn you into a puppet cowboy before it kills you.

He insisted we called him "Dan the Manager"—not "Dan."

"I always carry a gun, and it's impossible to get the drop on me," Dan the Manager would say as we'd open the snack bar for the twelve thirty matinee. Then he'd round the corner to the projection booths. Gary Jay, an usher and steroid abuser (he wasn't ever going to grow taller than the four foot nine God gave him, so why not?), would hop out like a demented gnome, brandish a Goody comb like a pistol, and scream, *"Bang-you're-dead-Dan!"*

Dan would chuckle through clenched molars, mutter something that sounded like "Y'tried that in T'xs you'd git a winder in yer head"* and then vanish into his "office"—a lawn chair behind one of the platter projectors. The he'd crack the cap on another bottle of liver eraser and we'd get to work bringing the magic of Hollywood to Northern Virginia.

The first matinee would end. The afternoon crowd, sun-blind from swimming or footsore from shopping, would

---

*I'm pretty sure that's what it was. But maybe he was saying, "You pry that princess faggot grin off of your head." Or maybe he was a secret film scholar and was saying, "Dwight Frye was a nexus for wilder cinema." If the third is correct, then I had a hand in tormenting a quiet genius.

be gathering at the upstairs box office. Dan the Manager had long ago drifted into whatever slushy Chuck Norris dreamscape the vodka took him to. Gary Jay and I couldn't handle the swelling masses alone. Who would rise to take the reins at the Towncenter 3? Who would push through the double glass doors of the street-level entrance and stomp his way down the stairs, like Gene Simmons and Wilt Chamberlain about to set a basement full of uppity pussy straight?

No one. No one came from street level. Help was already in the Towncenter 3. Its name was Roddy, and it lived there.

Roddy the assistant manager lived in the theater. He'd emptied out one of the supply closets. He'd installed an inflatable mattress, a Shower Anywhere portable shower, and a wee television. He slept amid the powdered-butter fumes and empty drink-syrup tanks. He had grub-white skin and Goth circles under his eyes that, unlike those of Goths, came from really, truly existing half in the world of the dead. He smelled like carpeting, Scotch tape, and steak sauce. He was almost forty but had one of those half mustaches that thirteen-year-olds have. He was the closest thing to a zombie I've yet encountered in this world.

But even zombies have basic drives—see, move, kill, eat. Roddy had those, with an occasional command to bathe. He also had an overriding drive to get everyone in the concession line "snacked and soda'ed," as he'd say. It was the one time he had grace and beauty. If only a woman of patience could have been down there during that fifteen-minute window when he was dispensing Sno-

Caps and buttering popcorn,* maybe she'd have taken him by his velour sleeve, walked him up into the sunlight and away from his rickety shower and pool-raft bed, and rescued her zombie husband. Alas. *Alas!*

So once the crowds had dispersed and the platter projectors were humming, it was time for a weekly game called What Benign Thing Will Make Roddy Explode?

Gary Jay and I and the two other ushers who came on for the afternoon shift—Bryan and Trace—would quietly do our jobs and engage Roddy in pleasant chitchat. However, our chitchat was the opening gambit in our ongoing social experiment:

"Hey, Roddy, I heard only homos come from Carlisle, Pennsylvania." (Roddy was from Carlisle, as he often told us.)

Roddy would grin as he inventoried Junior Mints. "People say that because we've got the Redskins training camp."

"Huh. That's interesting. You know what else is interesting? The way only homos listen to Deep Purple." (Deep Purple was Roddy's favorite band, and he was fond of cranking "Perfect Strangers" on the tape deck of his perpetually out-of-commission car in the parking lot late at night.)

Roddy would crack open a roll of nickels into the nickel well of the register and say, "Actually, Deep Purple's about the only non-homo music left in the world."

"Roddy, you smell like a corpse fart, you have no penis, and you should kill yourself. And you're a homo."

---

*Fill it halfway, two squirts of butter-flavored oil, fill it the rest of the way, three more squirts.

Roddy would wink and say, "Sticks and stones."

"Hey, Roddy, I had a banana for breakfast."

Roddy would slam the counter with his pasty forearms and shriek, "A ba-NANA? They're for monkeys to eat! You saying I want to eat a BANANA? What are you saying? You think I can't walk it? Huh? Ol' Roddy, living at the Towncenter 3? YOU THINK I CAN'T WALK IT, MR. CREAM SODA?"

Then we'd descend to theater level and corral the matinee audience out and the afternoon audience in while Roddy continued screaming. If any of the patrons asked what the noise was, we'd say it was the *Jaws* movie, that the shark was eating an old hobo. More than one kid, waiting to see *Benji the Hunted* or *Adventures in Babysitting*, would turn to their parents and say, "I want to go see a shark eat a hobo!"

The early evening shows saw me in the ticket booth, scamming half stubs. Scamming half stubs was a wonderful, entry-level criminal activity wherein you'd sell a ticket, tear it in half (the Towncenter 3 couldn't afford to pay a separate ticket taker) and then sell the *other* half to the next customer. You'd pocket the second customer's admission money.

You couldn't do this with something no one was coming to see, like *Who's That Girl?* or *Summer School*. But if we got something like *The Living Daylights* or *Coming to America?* Those movies provided enough half stubs to purchase a few cases of beer, plus a bottle or two of Mad Dog 20/20—Bryan and Trace's favorite. On days when they wouldn't work, and we had some random "floater" filling in or training on the platters, I'd pocket all the half-stub money. I was a thief. I spent the money on books and music. I stole from a struggling three-plex movie theater to expand my cultural horizons.*

So once the early evening tickets were sold—or, better yet, the weekend matinee tickets—I'd curl up on the floor and put R.E.M.'s *Fables of the Reconstruction*† on my cassette player and read Philip K. Dick's *The Man in the High Castle*.

> Called the fool and the company
> On his own where he'd rather be
> —R.E.M., "Maps and Legends"

The Man in the High Castle is an alternate-history SF novel about an America where the Axis powers have won World War II. And *Fables of the Reconstruction* is an album with songs about falling asleep while reading,

---

*I'd purchase my music two doors down from the Towncenter 3 at a record store called Waxie Maxie's, at which I used to work; they justifiably fired me after I mouthed off to a customer who berated me for not finding the Energizer battery refund coupons fast enough for his liking. By that point, I was cool with it—I couldn't take listening to another spin of Jean Beauvoir's *Drums Along the Mohawk* or Tears for Fears's *Songs from the Big Chair*, abiding staff favorites.

My books I'd purchase at a hobby store where I used to get my D&D books and lead figurines. I stopped going when, my senior year of high school, I casually mentioned to the kindly proprietor that I was going to college. His eyes went stony and he said, "You going to go learn how to wipe your ass without getting shit on your pants?" "What?" I asked, and then he bent down over his painted orcs and umberhulks and muttered, "Don't *ever* come back here again." And I never did.

† Yeah, I know, music snob. That's what I call it, so there.

16

trains and locomotion, and movement—and, by impli-
cation, escape and transformation—plus cryptic, advi-
sory screeds. Also eccentrics, weirdos, loners, and failing
romances charted by passing comets.*

So, while Michael Stipe's voice soared through
"Kohoutek" or "Good Advices" and the setting sun
knifed through the cracks in the pulled ticket-window
shade, I read. I read about a North American continent
sliced up by the victorious Germans, Japanese, and Ital-
ians. I read about the shell-shocked Americans, inhabiting
the gloomy, tense, unfeeling, and defeated country.

> The hills ringing hear the words in time
> Listen to the holler, listen to my walls within my tongue
> Can't you see you made my ears go tin?
> The air quicken tension building inference suddenly
> Life and how to live it
> —R.E.M., "Life and How to Live It"

And now I saw Sterling differently. Now, with the sterile, pitiless prose of Philip K. Dick and the oblique, teasing
music and lyrics of *Fables of the Reconstruction* clang-
ing around the too-tight tent of my mind and its limited
experiences, I saw how beautiful my suburb was, like an
accidental poem.

---

*The guys in R.E.M. don't have a lot of good things to say about *Fables*.
Too bad, guys—it changed my life. And I know I misinterpreted a lot of
these lyrics to suit my purposes at the time, but it ceased being your album
the minute I "bought" it. Empires have been built on *Electric Youth*, I bet.

(I've been there I know the way)
Can't get there from here
—R.E.M., "Can't Get There from Here"

If I could finally see, at the right angles (or during magic hour or in the summer moonlight), that even the strip mall that held the Towncenter 3 had majesty in it, how would I feel if I ever reached San Francisco, London, the Hebrides? My frustration and hatred of Sterling got me nowhere. It wasn't until I started loving it that I was on the way to leaving. And it wasn't until I relaxed with a good book and terrific music that I got the first buzz of restlessness.

Pay for your freedom, find another gate
Guilt by associate, the rushes wilted a long time ago
Guilty as you go
—R.E.M., "Green Grow the Rushes"

I couldn't see any of this then. It's only now, as I write it, on another coast, that I see what the time in the echo chamber of a ticket booth did. There were future musicians standing at the back of Fugazi shows, watching the band and the crowd and drinking in the pulsing thrum. They galvanized their identities while, at the same time, they bled faceless into the crowd, the band, the walls, and the memory of the evening.

The book and the cassette tape—they did the same thing for me. People will find transformation and transcendence in a McDonald's hash brown if it's all they've got. Come to think of it, I bet I'd be a better writer if my portal had been a hash brown. Oh well. Don't look back.

Before the Towncenter 3, I imagined I would get married and stay in Sterling and try to become a writer there, the way Stephen King never left Maine and wrote his novels on a washing machine in the trailer he shared with his growing family. Or John Waters, changing cinema forever without leaving Baltimore. It had been done before. I had my examples. I could justify my immobility.

> At least it's something you've left behind
> Like Kohoutek you were gone
> —R.E.M., "Kohoutek"

Of course, "justify my immobility" was just "fool myself" with exactly triple the syllables. Listening to *Fables of the Reconstruction* got me close to this realization only for as long as I listened to the album. Eventually I'd wander downstairs and watch five minutes of Michael Caine fighting a giant rubber shark and wondering why, after *Blame It on Rio,* he'd returned to the tropics. At least the last time there'd been underage sex dangled in front of him. Now there was an inert fish prop and Mario Van Peebles. Then again, to do a classic like *Get Carter* he had to endure the gray grime gut-punch of Newcastle. Fuck it—I'd probably opt for the shitty shark film in the sunshine over . . . and by that point, the memory of whatever I'd gotten close to, up in the ticket booth? Gone.

At the end of the day
I'll forget your name . . .
—R.E.M., "Good Advices"

In a few years all of these certainties would be burned to useless wicks, and I'd be making my way out and over. First into Washington, DC, doing punishing open mikes as a comedian, and then west west west as the stand-up scene crumbled. It was all part of my plan (I said to myself) to eventually end up a writer. If writing for *Gent* magazine led Stephen King to *The Stand,* then emceeing a weekend at Sir Laffs a Lot would lead to my writing this boss novel I had in my head about a dude who battles mutants in a wasteland. At least my time at Sir Laffs a Lot, Quackers, and the Comedy Factory Outlet* would provide the shotgun-wielding hero of my wasteland epic some kick-ass quips as he blew slippery chunks out of scabrous mutants. See? I had it all worked out.

He was reared to give respect
But somewhere down the line he chose
To whistle as the wind blows
—R.E.M., "Wendell Gee"

I was an idiot. It was my first attempt at a Plan. For Life. And How to Live It. I refined it in the coming years. Until then, it would be self-contradicting confusion and an adherence to the routines and safety of the suburbs.

*All real names, all real places.

20

The walls are built up, stone by stone
The fields divided one by one
—R.E.M, "Driver 8"

"Feeling Gravitys Pull" started up—I still remember this so clearly—at the moment in *The Man in the High Castle* when Mr. Tagomi is looking at that little pin—the Frank Frink artifact with the "satori" form on it—and he hallucinates an alternate reality where the Germans *lost* World War II, and he's in San Francisco. Michael Stipe was singing about falling asleep but still reading every paragraph. Perfect immersion in a book.

I had to go back and reread the page a few times. As I read it, I kept drifting out of the book, out of the booth, and coasting on the green crest of the song, to the momentary idea that any point on Earth was mine for the visiting, that I'd lucked out living in the reality I was in. And I also got the feeling I was souring and damaging that luck by enjoying the contentment of pulling the shades on the sun, and shutting out my fellow employees and the world, and folding myself up in the construct of a brilliant novel like *The Man in the High Castle,* that all the reading I'd been doing up to this point hadn't enhanced my life, but rather had replaced and delayed it. I'm describing it better than the half lick I tasted in the gloom of the ticket booth.

If I see myself I see you
—R.E.M., "Old Man Kensey"

And then it was gone. I tried to make it come back—not by shutting off the tape and bursting out of the booth to walk around and watch people interact with each other. I replayed the song and reread the passage. Nothing. You can't stage an epiphany. All I got were random pieces and half-complete ideas.

I looked up at the glowing rectangle of the pulled shade and tried to become pure mind.

And that's when Bryan barged into the booth, excited, huffing from flying up the flight of stairs from the snack bar.

"Roddy's out of his room, somewhere. It's . . . come see what's under his mattress!"

I ran downstairs to see.

"Well, I want the throwing stars," said Gary Jay before anyone else spoke.

Trace was standing, holding the air mattress like a surfboard. On the floor, where it once lay, were three air pistols, five throwing stars, two throwing knives, and a pair of nunchakus. I subconsciously panned my eyes along the weapons, left to right, like the scene in *Escape from New York* where the camera pans along the equipment Kurt Russell's going to take into the New York City Penal Colony to save the president.

After Gary spoke, no one else did. We all, wordlessly, bent down and took things. I took an air pistol (it looked like a revolver). Bryan took another air pistol—it looked like a 1911 Colt .45—and the nunchakus. Gary Jay swooped up the throwing stars and Trace took the third pistol. It wasn't modeled after any existing gun. It just looked like a generic air pistol—vaguely ray gun–y, brown grips and black barrel. Trace laid the air mattress down and we all left.

I rushed back up to the ticket booth and lifted the shade. Now we were in the magic hour, when the evening customers would start drifting up. They'd appear in groups of two or three, then in a brief, chaotic mass, which would quickly form a line. I put the air pistol in the drawer and got the three spools of tickets ready in their dispensers for the evening's shows.

Huh. Thick crowd early for *The Living Daylights*. I prepared, mentally, to start selling half stubs when I saw, over the heads of the people in line, Roddy.

He was standing in the parking lot, leaning against the primer-paint derelict of his car, holding court in front of some prepubescent metalheads. He was trying hard to act bored, rolling his eyes and shaking his head in that sad, "You poor, uncultured idiot" way, where you want to assert dominance without saying anything startling or original. Roddy could only do this with twelve-year-olds. Anyone who'd experienced real heartache, traveled outside of the Sterling city limits, or read any book above the Young Adult genre never doled out more than fifteen seconds of regard for Roddy. This was where he got to wear his "old sage" costume. In the parking lot of a strip mall, lit by mustardy streetlamps, bracketed by the Giant Foods, Hunan Garden, a real estate office, karate and pizza and Waxie Maxie's and the Towncenter 3—forever dropping vague hints about buying cigarettes or booze for kids who dreamed of someday, somehow, becoming Roddy. Soon they'd be the withholders of Pabst Blue Ribbon and Camels. They imagined pimple-ringed eyes looking up at them in wonder and imagined that Dire Straits's "Money for Nothing" would play whenever they walked.

But then Roddy nodded and pointed at one of the kids, and the *kid* produced a Camel hard pack and let Roddy bum a cig. Roddy stuck it in his mouth and then gestured—two more? Can I get two more for later? But the kid closed the pack. No dice. Maybe if we get some beer going later, he seemed to say.

And it hit me—I stole this poor bastard's BB pistol. The dude owned an air mattress, a bottle of shampoo, and three shirts. Hell, *I'd* want weapons, however useless, if I slept in the closet of a movie theater.

I looked in the doorway and Trace was standing there, looking as stricken as I felt. We didn't say anything to each other, but there it was, hanging in the air between us. Why had we stolen nine of the maybe sixteen possessions that Roddy owned?

"You wanna put 'em back?"

I said, "I do," almost before he could finish. I slipped the BB pistol into his hands, out of range of a woman's gaze, waiting to buy her ticket to see Timothy Dalton take on the ultimate Bond villain—Joe Don Baker.

"See you downstairs later."

I said, "Is Bryan putting his back?"

"He already did," said Trace. "I'm going to go talk to Gary Jay."

The first customers pressed against the ticket booth,

and I mentally calculated how many half tickets I could sell.

The last show of the night was at nine thirty. Once I bagged the receipts and wrote the gross in ballpoint pen in the separate brown paper bags, I closed the booth. I had $80 in my pocket from half stubs. I headed downstairs, to where Roddy was Windexing the glass top of the snack bar.

"You wanna go on a beer run?" I asked.

"What's everyone want?"

Trace came out of the projection booth. He'd probably just rolled Dan onto his belly so he wouldn't choke on vomit. He said, "Get the one bottle of Mad Dog 20/20. Or something strong like that. And then a case of beer? Pabst Blue Ribbon?"

"I don't want to carry a case back by myself. Someone come with me," said Roddy. "Gary Jay."

"He should usher *Adventures in Babysitting,*" said Trace, a little too quickly. "There's a bunch of middle school douchebags got dropped off by their parents down there."

"Well shit, you're still on cleanup." Roddy turned to me. "You come. You wait outside the Giant Foods. I'll get two twelve-packs; we'll carry those back."

I looked at Trace. He was trying to look bland and nonchalant and he was burning a lot of calories doing it.

"Yeah, I'll go. Okay." Roddy and I started toward the stairs leading to the street. Right before I turned the corner to follow Roddy, I saw Trace pivot and bolt downstairs, to the theaters.

* * *

"I'm being cool about it, but one of you assholes stole some of my shit," said Roddy abruptly. We were passing by the big, carved wooden lions in front of the Hunan Garden. The lions' scoop-jawed, toothy grins seemed to mock Roddy, who, even now, speaking through clenched teeth, looked like his droopy lower lip would slide and puddle onto the front of his shirt.

"Someone in the theater?"

"No, someone in the Pentagon, fuck-neck," said Roddy. "I went in for a second, to get some Freshen-up gum I'd stashed in my *Back to the Future* vest, and some of my shit was gone."

"What stuff?"

"Like you don't know."

I said, "I don't. Really. I don't know what you keep in there."

Roddy didn't say anything for a second. We were at the automatic doors for the Giant Foods.

"You almost slipped up there. See, if you'd said, 'I didn't take any of your throwing stars,' I'd know you were lying."

"Someone took—you have throwing stars?"

"Five of 'em. And I'm a dead shot throwing them. I've got air pistols, and Bruce Lee sticks, but no one took any of them," said Roddy, half to the air around us, like he was putting together a puzzle. "So I'm looking for someone with quick arms. Which you don't have."

I said, "Okay."

"See, I'm better'n Columbo at figuring this stuff out."

And then he stepped backward through the hissing-open doors, unable to suppress a girlish half chuckle as the doors opened as he'd hoped they would and he didn't bounce his ass on glass after uttering his exit line.

On our way back, Roddy expounded on *Columbo,* which was his favorite show. I realized, just before we reached the theater, that Roddy believed Columbo had a trained owl.

The last patrons climbed the stairs to the surface and home. Now it was us and Roddy.

Deep Purple's *Perfect Strangers* album was blasting through the sound system. Usually, before we started drinking, one of us would run to the tape machine, to try to slap a Van Halen or Hüsker Dü cassette in before Roddy could put in his beloved Deep Purple and claim the soundtrack for the evening. Now, in a misguided attempt to placate Roddy, someone had put in Deep Purple. But the Deep Purple cassette was in Roddy's room, nestled in its slot in his cassette carrier, among his .38 Special and Eagles and Jimmy Buffett tapes. So already, he knew that, again, someone had ransacked his stuff.

At least, Columbo would have guessed that.

Roddy placed his twelve-pack on the snack counter. I hurried downstairs, to hide the other one behind the last row of seats in theater one, our designated drinking area. Roddy would use his twelve-pack to entice his court of paint huffers and skate rats down into the theater, so we'd learned to stash our own. Roddy made friends with thirsty burnouts.

When I arrived back at the snack bar, Trace and Bryan were shotgunning beers. Roddy was slowly sipping his, still holding the bottle of MD 20/20.

"Where's Gary Jay?" I asked.

"Yeah, where is that strong-armed little fucker?" asked Roddy. "You'd think he'd—"

And then Melinda came around the corner, from the stairs leading up to the street.

Melinda restocked the salad bar at the Giant Foods and was currently having a sloppy romance with Bryan. She was still in high school but heading toward senior year. She was gap-toothed and apple-cheeked, but it all hung together as "cute." Bryan, vaguely dropping hints that he'd someday join the army and maybe become a Green Beret, hid his blazing, doomed passion for Melinda with a gruff nonchalance.

"Hey, guys," said Melinda.

"Yeah, what's up? Huh," said Bryan, sipping his beer to hide the smile that cracked his face.

Roddy looked pissed. You could tell he'd had something sinister and threatening in the breech, and Melinda had queered his pitch with her dopey cheerfulness. Melinda slid her shoulder under Bryan's free arm and tickled his stomach.

This was dark territory for Roddy. Two obviously innocent fellow employees—my stammering and buddy-buddy eagerness on the beer run had crossed me off the suspect list, and Trace's big, open face was a window into his crammed-with-facts, college-bound brain. My love of R.E.M. and science fiction were two more strikes against me. Roddy couldn't conceive I possessed the boldness of thievery with such mama's-boy tastes.

And, worst of all, there was Bryan, sharing the warmth of a female.

"Yyyyyyeah. Well, I'm going up, get my buds." Roddy grimaced as he killed his beer, placed the MD 20/20 on the counter, and mounted the stairs, off to collect his low-protein minions.

"Naw, I'm not giving them back," said Gary Jay. "He can't even prove I've got 'em."

Trace said, "Who else would steal 'em? Someone came in to see a movie, and then they went into his room . . . ?"

"Maybe." Gary Jay, Trace, and I were in the projection booth. The muffled sound of Deep Purple's "Wasted Sunsets" thrummed through the walls. Dan's carpeted snoring was louder.

"Man, the dude's such a psycho. He's up there with his dickhead friends; you can go put 'em back now," I said. Maybe I whined.

"He *acts* like a psycho."

I said, "What difference does that make?"

My guts were gnarled with this unpleasant feeling of fear, and then anger at myself for being afraid, and then guilt. If Gary Jay went down, it would be only because he got caught. I had a sneaking suspicion that Bryan, Trace, and I—compared to Gary Jay—were pussies. If he'd put the throwing stars back, I could erase some of that. An hour ago I was boring a hole through my limited suburban existence, catching a glimpse of the larger world.

Now I was begging my friend to preserve the lame-ass status quo. The next few years of my life—all through college, actually—would be a cursive progression: a huge loop forward and then a frantic, straight line back.

"Well, I tried," said Trace, like he'd carved it on a fresh tombstone. He walked away, defiantly, out of the projection booth and down the stairs into theater one for a fresh beer.

I took two seconds too long in thinking of something equally final and self-absolving to say. Roddy kicked the door open.

Behind him I could see four of his runty associates. It was as if Roddy were Dr. Moreau but, instead of trying to turn animals into men, he'd tried growing new versions of himself out of trimmings from his wispy mustache. Each of his burnout satellites was attempting to grow the same piebald caterpillar under his nose. The experiment wasn't a success, however—none of the runts had Roddy's dark circles under their eyes.

"Where's my fucking throwing stars?" Roddy was jutting his jaw as far forward as he could. The rerouting of energy made his belly sag. He only had so much to go around.

"In my pocket, next to my dick," said Gary Jay. One of the runts went, "Whoop!" You could tell Roddy couldn't figure out if Gary Jay was questioning his manhood. Was this a twisted, homophobic Labor of Hercules—recover your weapons by sucking my cock?

"Why'd you take 'em?"

Gary Jay said, "'Cause I wanted 'em. They're badass."

"You're right," said Roddy, as if conceding a point in an argument. "Why didn't you take the air pistols? Or the nunchakus?"

Then he turned on me, as quick and close to an adder striking as his starchy constitution could muster. "Were you gonna take my guns?"

"We were all in there," said Gary Jay. "But he and those other guys pussed out."

Roddy turned back to Gary Jay.

Somewhere, in that moment, there was a historic concert happening for two hundred people in a tiny room. Somewhere a band like Fugazi or Minor Threat was building its legacy. Somewhere a young filmmaker was sitting in a rep theater, watching *The Fallen Idol* or *The Red Shoes* and deciding, in their mind, to be an artist. Above me, in the ticket booth, was a book and a cassette of music I was trying to lash together as some sort of life raft to my future.

But right then, I only wanted one thing in the world. I wanted a guy to return five throwing stars to a guy he'd stolen them from, and avoid seeing something ugly, so I could go drink cheap beer and listen to mid-career Deep Purple.

Finally, Roddy turned back to me. "Ha! Yeah! You *did* puss out!"

Then, as if illustrating to his Acne Legion that true power lies in giving it away, he swiveled his gaze back to Gary Jay and said, "Keep 'em, I don't give a fart. They're not balanced right anyway."

Holy shit, I had to get out of Virginia.

Hours later, wrapped in a tingly overcoat of beer and

sweet wine, I sat in theater one. *Perfect Strangers* had been playing, nonstop, the entire time, but we were beyond caring. We'd broken out the BB pistols and, in a ritual we repeated almost every night from that point on, we shot at Roddy's minions. That was the price they paid for the alcohol they drank. They'd stand down in front of the screen and let us ding them with metal BBs.

Trace and Gary Jay sat together, aiming each shot. I was firing the 1911-style gun one-handed and missing. The booze wasn't helping. Out of a dimly remembered mercy we aimed only for the torso.

Roddy sat next to me, explaining in detail how he'd solved the mystery of the throwing stars. Normally I'd have been annoyed, but the sheer level of bullshit in his story—he actively disremembered conceding the throwing stars to Gary Jay and was planning on ambushing him with nunchakus later—delighted me.

Bryan and Melinda were behind us, doing the kind of frantic tongue-kissing that made it look like they were each eating a peach.* The scruffy punks, air-guitaring—badly—to "Under the Gun," were now absorbing head shots. But, armored with bellies full of fortified wine, they were beyond sense or concern. Another night at the Towncenter 3—a night that never really started—was about to not really end.

---

*Oh man, but did Melinda ever break poor Bryan's heart. He proposed a few years later, after washing out of the army, and she called it off a week before the nuptials. I ran into her, years later, at college, at an R.E.M. concert. They were touring on the *Document* album. I guess she took a lyric from "Auctioneer," off of *Fables of the Reconstruction,* to heart—"She didn't want to get pinned down by her prior town."

I still think about the Towncenter 3, some nights before sleep. I imagine floating above an all-ages show at the Birchmere in Washington, DC. Fugazi is cutting a swath of gut-bucket fury through space and time. I was never there. But like Roddy, I can re-remember things to suit my regret.

Then, in my memory, I float northwest to the suburbs, to Sterling, and over the Towncenter 3.

And then I begin descending down, down, underground. Past Gary Jay, painting the men's room with regal purple MD 20/20 vomit. Past Dan, sleeping on his side and muttering about riding the high country. Past Bryan and Melinda, sharing Junior Mints at the snack bar, outlined by a heart they couldn't see was already broken. Then over to Roddy's office, where Trace restole the nunchakus.

And finally, down to theater one, where a cocky corpse named Roddy shot skate punks with a BB gun.

Where's our coffee-table book? Oh, wait. No one took pictures. And we were all ugly.

Punch-Up Notes

Scott—

   I'm going to start with three big, overall ideas for the movie, and then go through scene by scene. And these notes are based on the fourth draft, which Kyle and Kaitlin wrote after Interrupt-ials came out, and they had to change the third act location from a water park to a go-kart track.

Patton

3/11/2011

YOU MAY MISS THE BRIDE

Fourth draft notes

First off, I think the character of *Tracey*, the bride, is wildly inconsistent. It almost seems like her condition changes to fit the joke needed for each scene.

   Once we establish that she gets amnesia from eating the bad sushi at the bachelorette party in the opening scene, we need to stick to that. She wouldn't remember that her mom queefs whenever she hears a saxophone playing, so there's no reason for her to get nervous when the jazz combo gets ready to play at the bridal shower. I know there's a series of laughs that follow from her kicking the sax player in the scrotum to stop him coming in on that jazzy version of "The Lady in Red"—the band mistaking his screams as a signal to play "It's Raining Men," and then his vomiting in the trumpet, and then Tracey's dog shitting all over itself when the trumpet player plays his first note and sprays vomit all over the dog. It's a funny, quirky, captivating sequence, but we need to find a less sweaty way for Tracey to suddenly and without warning attack a musician's nutsack. Also, "The Lady in Red" might be expensive.

But that's just one example of how we need consistency in her amnesia. I like how the neurosurgeon explains how even though she doesn't remember that she's *getting* married, or who's she's getting married to, the fact that she *wants* to be married, in a general sense, still holds up. Make sure to indicate in the script that the neurosurgeon should be sitting in front of one of those light-box displays of Tracey's brain, so it looks more authentic to the audience.

But let's make sure there are enough reasons for her to shrug those adorable shoulders and soldier ahead with the big day. The fact that the groom is good-looking and is sweet and smart and truly cares for her certainly helps. And when he shows her that he's running that halfway house for rehabilitated criminals, and she can see from the picture in her locket that her dad was once in prison, because there she is visiting him as a little girl.

Which brings me to the father character. I don't think he should have been sent to prison for burning all those people alive and then masturbating when the cops showed up. Yes, it was the late seventies, and it was a disco, but I think the whole "disco sucks" thing is completely played out at this point—does anyone even care and, what's more, does today's audience even remember when disco was? It puts such a pall over the proceedings. You've got this series of funny scenes, and then each one gets spoiled by the mention of the father's crime. For instance:

The karaoke scene, where the CD gets stuck, and Tracey and Paul, the groom, have to sing "Knock Three Times" like twenty times. The smash cut, when we realize they've been singing for so long, is funny. But then when the CD is finally fixed, and they walk offstage, the mom (who's now drunk; it's always funny when an old lady gets drunk) says, "That sounded worse than the screams of all those people being burned slowly alive while your dad masturbated in the moonlight of that parking lot."

The scene where *Paul's friend bumps up against the wedding cake,* and instead of collapsing it gets smooshed to the side and ends up looking like a gigantic penis. I like the Aerosmith "Big Ten Inch Record" music cue, but then Tracey says that weird line, "I wonder if my father's penis looked like that while he tugged on it maniacally while all of those people died in agony."

Then there's that weird moment right at the beginning of the third act. On the beach, *when the sea lion has stolen the bride's veil,* and Tracey and Paul are trying to coax it in to shore? The seal somehow gets the veil on its head, and Paul says, "I'll bet the people who died in that disco hallucinated something like that as they were overcome by fumes."

I could list at least five other examples—the water park scene with the enema bag, the montage of trying on dresses, the three-legged race, the ex-cons doing yoga— where someone graphically and deliberately brings up the father's horrific past crime. Did one of the writers have a parent or relative who did something like that—or did *exactly* that? It's so specific. I understand wanting to make amends to the public for something someone in your family did, but a comedy like *You May Miss the Bride* might not be the place.

Here is a list of better crimes for the father to have committed. They're the sort of fun "movie crimes" that a more roguish character would commit, so that the audience might still like him:

Car theft
Stole receipts from a concert (*not* from a benefit)
Smuggling a wacky animal
Drove beer across state lines on a bet
Sold moonshine or fun drugs (not coke and not heroin)
Robbed a rich douchebag's house
Ripped off the mob
Stole a blimp

Another big note is *Tracey's gay best friend.*
I don't want to be insulting, but the character of Sebas-

tian Plush is written as if the writer has never met or seen a gay person. Do we get any laughs from his being a flamingo tamer beyond the first joke, where the flamingo jabs its beak into the minister's crotch?

Also, I don't know why the font for all of Sebastian's lines is suddenly Lucinda Calligraphy, where the rest of the script is just plain old Courier. And all these music cues—is a different Abba song going to play *every* time Sebastian appears? I'm just thinking that's going to be very expensive. Maybe just pick one Abba song, and that's the one that plays? We go through half of *Abba Gold* and we're not even out of the first act yet.

So keep that in mind as I go through, pretty much scene by scene. I'll try to suggest some better lines of dialogue, maybe some tweaking and scene rearranging. Final discretion is with the screenwriters and producers, of course.

Opening scene: When the girls are piling into the limo for the bachelorette party, have one of them try to poke her head through the open sunroof before the sunroof is open. Kinda bump her head, like we know how lame a person yelling through a sunroof is, so we're going to do this clever, postmodern take on it first. The audience will really appreciate that.

Or could Tracey do that? Foreshadowing?

At the sushi restaurant: First off, change the name of the sushi restaurant from Hong Kong Fish to something like, I don't know, Tokyo Raw?

When the sushi chefs yell at the girls when they come in, they should be friendly. Sushi chefs are usually saying a greeting, not threatening people.

Some bachelorette gift ideas: I think you should pick just one dildo-related gift. As it stands now, you've got a dildo hat, dildo coffee mug (how would that even work?), dildo champagne stems, a dog bed made of dildos, and, finally, just a huge black dildo that the one girl waves around. My comedy instincts tell me to just go with the one huge black dildo.

Also, when she's waving it around, maybe it can slip out of her hand and fall into someone's miso soup? (DO NOT have her say "Me so sorry!") Or it could fall perfectly in the middle of a sushi platter. I would save this gag for the end of the scene—it would be an elegant way to button the scene and lead us out of it. Keep this in mind as I go through the other beats.

Okay, so—bachelorette gifts (big black dildo), the going-around-the-table-and-revealing-one-embarassing-but-funny-thing-about-the-bride (only one "She has crazy periods" joke), and then the bad sushi, then the bride passes out. Oh, and then the big black dildo lands either in the soup or on a platter, and then we're out. (The Shania Twain "Man! I Feel Like a Woman!" music cue should probably begin the scene—I don't think it will play well over a big black dildo.)

Note: I would strongly suggest *not* having Sebastian Plush in this scene. He flirts with the one sushi chef, whom we never see again, and his line "Eda-mama like!" is too sweaty.

The hospital room: Tracey wakes up; doesn't recognize Paul; diagnosis.

So we establish that Tracey doesn't recognize Paul,

her groom. And that she doesn't remember she's getting married.

Would she be sharing a room with someone at this point? I mean, she just collapsed and is under observation. I understand why the other patient is there—an old man yelling for a bedpan and farting is a nice counterpoint to the tenderness and concern that Paul is showing Tracey—but, given what's coming (the vomit-and-shit chain at the bridal shower, and all the groin trauma, and the hamster flying up the dog's butt), I think we can allow ourselves a little breathing room. I really wish *Fart School* hadn't made so much money last summer.

The doctor's explanation is good (remember—light box!), so here's my suggestion as to why Tracey decides to go ahead with this marriage to a guy who, ostensibly, is a stranger:

I know how I wrote, at the beginning of these notes, how she sees what an amazing guy Paul is.

But what if there's something more fundamental, and *internal,* about her that makes her decide to go along with the wedding? About how now, with a more or less clean slate in her head, she grasps how miraculous even the smallest incidents in life can be, and that something as silly and pedestrian as a marriage can be as bold and startling an adventure as wandering the globe or creating a great piece of art, and that it only matters how curious and committed each marriage partner is in themselves?

Also, when the doctor walks out, only have one of his feet inside a poop-smeared bedpan.

Page 11 The grandmother, and not the niece, should say, "That monkey's an asshole."

Page 16 When the car backs over the wedding planner's foot, she should throw her notebook in the air instead of dropping it.

Page 17 Only one photo of the groom's bare scrotum should make it into the slide show.

Page 21 Change the line "We've got more guests than a Serbian gang bang" to "Our guest list is longer than Grandma's boobs."

Page 24 You should be able to hear Paul's friend grunting through the Starbucks bathroom door, but not pooping.

Page 31 Foreshadow that the seal likes frilly things by having it try to take a bite of Sebastian's assless lace shorts.

Page 34 When Paul is serenading Tracey below her window, have the bird shit on him when he tries to sustain that long note in "Unchained Melody" (in the mouth?).

Page 38 A ghost is too far-fetched at this point. Make it a crazy homeless dude.

Page 41 If the mom's going to queef during the parade, make the queefs in time to the marching band's song.

Page 44 Fat triplets is funnier than fat twins.

Page 48 Lee Majors cameo instead of Tony Danza?

Page 55 When the best man falls off the roof, have him land in a truck hauling liposuctioned fat instead of mattresses.

Page 60 Put roller skates on the dad, a sombrero on the mom, and add an incontinent pug.

Page 61–108 This is all perfect, except for when the bride says, "You wanna get out of here? You talk to me . . . ," which is from *The Road Warrior*.

Final scene: After the jerry-rigged wedding in the parking lot, when Tracey and Paul kiss, and his kiss restores her memory? I like that. Then he says that sweet line, "Let's make new memories," and then she laughs, but then she says, still laughing: "As long as I can someday forget the horrific image of my dad's strained, joyous face as he reached orgasm outside that burning disco full of shrieks and death." Not only is it a weird line to end a romantic comedy on, but then having the Trammps' "Disco Inferno" start playing is, I think, the absolutely wrong last idea for the audience to walk out of the theater with.

Please see my attached list of alternate last lines and appropriate songs to follow them with. I met Kid Rock at an MTV gifting suite last week, and he's excited about getting a song in the movie.

I couldn't be farther away from all of the snow in my life, geographically or mentally, than I am right now, as I write this.

I'm in Burbank, California—in the hot, yellow yolk of summer. July bakes the town like a corpse on desert asphalt. But it's Burbank asphalt, which means there's a Baskin-Robbins nearby.

The first memory I can remember as a memory is of snow. Looking out through the balcony window of my family's tiny Norfolk, Virginia, apartment in 1970 and seeing snow falling from the sky.

Except that's not how I saw it.

My fresh-from-the-oven toddler's eyes were fixed on the frame of the glass balcony door. And they must've thought the snow was stationary and the building was rising through the morning air into the sky.

My first coherent thought about life was that apartment houses could levitate in the snow. Decades later, when I took LSD in a tiny apartment in San Francisco, I had a realization. Most narcotics are designed to approximate the nonjudgmental, magically incorrect way we see the world before we can speak. Thus, the whorls in the wood on the cheap kitchen table swirled like tiny maelstroms. Of course—each of them was a twirly doorway into Tableland.

A row of action figures on a shelf subtly nodded their heads in time to Fleetwood Mac's "Don't Stop." They never got around to actually dancing—and how could they? The Fleetwood Mac song was playing from the television, where Bill Clinton and Al Gore and their wives danced woodenly, having just won the '92 election. Those poor action figures were embarrassed by the cut-string puppets on television. They could be posed to appear like they were fighting, riding motorcycles, firing fearsome weapons. And there, within plain sight—four humans with ten times the range of motion and strength, and they couldn't even dance to a Fleetwood Mac song.

Finally, I sat staring a row of books on a shelf while the dawn turned the room gray/gray-blue/blue/harsh/dry/tired. I saw the books as books, and then as distant vats of pulp waiting for pressing and ink, and farther back as a forest and then as scattered atoms, and the universe was a cold forest of cooling fire, waiting to become wood and pulp and books.

But I never even got close to thinking, during those twelve melty hours of hallucinating, that my apartment building could levitate. Only babies hallucinate at that level.

We're Playing Snow Fort

I'm eleven years old and my two friends are ten years old except for one other friend I have who is also eleven years old but is only twenty-two days older than me. And this is how cool our snow fort is:

First off, the back wall we didn't even have to build. The snowplows scraped their way through the streets early early early this morning and piled up big, packed walls of snow. So that became the back wall of the fort. It's probably fifty feet high, maybe. I can't jump over it, so that's probably fifty feet. Numbers are how you understand the world. Like, a dad makes a million dollars a year. Gum stays in your stomach for seven years. Only grandparents are allowed to buy special shirts that always have five pieces of candy in the pocket. And anything I can't jump over is fifty feet.

The snowfall, starting early in the evening the night before, stayed strong and did not weaken. The clock radio with the red glowing numbers (red numbers tell parents to go out and make money) next to our parents' bed emitted the Chuckling Voices and Fart Sounds. The Chuckling Voices said the schools of Loudoun County bowed in

47

fear when faced with the strength and steadfastness of the snowfall. The schools would close, out of respect for the icy onslaught from the sky. When they said our school's name, *two* fart sounds. Because we always close. Because the Mighty Snow must be respected.

We must be like the snowfall.

The Mighty Snow, which made our parents, so sure of our schedules and destinies, shake their heads and mutter, "Just great," when faced with the reality that the sky and snow and cold can decide a new path for our day. Somewhere, our teachers are crying and kicking things because they don't get to make us learn numbers and books full of dead people. And the principal is going, "Boo hoo hoo." Mighty Snow—you are more real a god than Jesus and the Hercules gods from school and whatever the Bergs, Steinbergs, and Axelrods say thanks to during their holidays. Those gods never show up. But the temperature gets cold and that's Mighty Snow's way of saying, "Soon, my minions. Soon, I will show you real strength and also you'll get a day off 'cause I'm so strong."

So we'll be strong like the snow. We'll be stronger than Trey and Paul from the far end of Crescent Court. We'll be stronger than Mike's older brother, who plays soccer but is fat and mean. And we will definitely be stronger than Mrs. Jeskyne, who yells and yells from her screen door. In the sunlight reflected off this new snow, wearing a nightshirt that says BORN TO SHOP and holding one of those weensy barbells she stomp-walks with, it is clear how slim and weak she is. Blond hair and tan skin like hers may have power on a beach somewhere. But here in the Northern Virginia snow? She is like if an aerobics lady tried to fight the big metal walkers on the planet Hoth, which Mike says are called AT-ATs, and then he'll tell you what each letter means like he's going to win a prize. Today, if Mrs. Jeskyne wants to yell at us, it will have to be over the fifty-foot front wall of the snow fort.

Around this we built the three other walls of the fort, growing out of the big, packed ice wall. So the fort faces my house, which is across from Mrs. Jeskyne's. If Trey and Paul and Mike's older brother and anyone else want to attack, they're going to have to come around the sides of my house. All they'd have to hide behind would be the hedges, which are so unleafy now because of the winter that we can throw the bigger snowballs right through them and *boom!* snow all over their faces, which is a total skeeze-mo.

The two side walls are high enough to climb over but not jump. Mike built a slide against the one wall, the one facing the driveway. Mike thinks everything should have an "escape hatch" or "escape pod" or something ever since seeing *Star Wars,* and that's how he broke his finger, trying to say that skateboard taped to his bike was an "escape pod" when we were racing down Tyler Street, which is steep. Thistle isn't something to escape into.

We've piled up enough snowballs to probably totally destroy anyone who comes our way. Like, if Mike's older brother took his sled and outfitted it with some cool kind of snow engine, and also some sort of robot cannon that could whirl around and fire like a million snowballs like a laser gun, we'd still take him out. It'd be totally cool if he were to come zooming along the street, banking on the piled-up snow like a James Bond car, and then suddenly jumped the wall with the sled, but we'd dodge him in slow motion and karate-throw snowballs at him while jumping and flipping to the side, still in slow motion like Steve Austin, and he'd be blown off the sled and we'd stand there, victorious, and then a snow yeti would attack and we'd save the neighborhood with our snowball skills and the cool rocket sled, which we'd now have through beating Mike's older brother, which is a rule of snowball fights. Mike says that probably won't happen but that we can definitely build a smaller version of the snow sled out of Legos and have it fight his action figures of the dudes in the bar in *Star Wars*. At least, the ones we didn't blow up with firecrackers out by the public pool last summer.

Trey and Paul are suddenly in the distance, shin-deep in the snow and looping toward us. They've got a paper bag and I'm sure it's full of some super ice ball and I tell Mike, "We've got company," like I saw Han Solo do once, and we get ready with a snowball in each hand and our stash of extra ammo on these cool shelves we cut out of the walls of the snow fort.

Now they're closer, and what looked like them coming toward us in the snow was really them walking right by us, looking over at the fort and our heads peeping over the side. They look confused and happy and tired. Trey gives Paul the paper bag and now I can see that they spray-painted their mouths silver, like they have only robot mouths. It's a cyborg attack!

"Halt, cyborg!" I yell.

They laugh but then they look scared and look down, as if to see if they're really cyborgs, for a second. Then they laugh again and all the laughing makes them have to stop and catch their breath. They each take a breath from the bag, which, maybe, since they're pretending to be cyborgs, holds special cyborg air.

"No cyborgs in our fort!" yells Mike.

Trey and Paul stare at us and don't say anything, and then Paul goes, "Boop beep beep," and they totally crack up. They each take another breath of cyborg air and start walking away.

That's when I see it—Mike's dad, creeping along the breezeway of Mrs. Jeskyne's house.

Mike's dad is really really cool. He's like a much bigger kid and not like a dad at all. He showed us how you can type numbers onto a calculator and then turn it upside down to form words. What would Dolly Parton be like if she were flat-chested? And he typed in 55378008 and turned it upside down and everyone was cracking up. Mike explained it to me later and I got it and when I tried to do it in music class I typed in 2s instead of 5s and it didn't work.

And Mike's dad is always helping us build with Legos and sometimes comes out and plays hide-and-seek and man he's the best hider. So I figure, he's taking the day off of work, and he's planning a cool frontal attack. I have to remember, after we totally blast him with snowballs, to have him show me the calculator trick again.

I look over and Mike isn't even holding a snowball. He's staring at his dad.

"Arm yourself!" I say. "This could be a trick."

Then Mrs. Jeskyne opens her front door, and Mike's dad shoves his way in, before she can look over his shoulder, looking back at us nervously before shutting the door behind him.

"You think he's going to go up on her roof, try to attack us from there?"

Mike says, "He's not going on the roof."

And then he starts *wrecking the fort*.

I can't think of anything to say. It's the greatest fort we've ever built and he's tearing it apart. I sit in one of the two command chairs we made out of snow and watch him kick the walls outward in pieces, saving the escape slide for last.

I realize he's under the control of the cyborgs and I let him run out his destructo program. When he's done he starts laughing and since we know Mike's brother isn't home we go to Mike's house and steal his VHS of *The Warriors* and watch it on the VCR. Mike's dad comes in when the Warriors are fighting the roller-skating guys in the subway, but he doesn't come in to say hi or tell us a joke. And when we get to the part where the guy says, "Warriors, come out to plaaaaa-aaaay!" Mike doesn't talk along with the movie like he usually does, which is weird 'cause it's his favorite part of any movie. Then I get out the huge box where Mike's got all these different Legos from different sets, and we start working on the snow sled. Mike starts working on the escape pod first and then gets frustrated because he makes it huge, bigger than the snow sled's ever going to be, 'cause he's using up all the pieces, and he says, "I want a huge escape pod." I say fine, but we'd better get the *Warriors* tape back to his brother's room, but Mike says who cares. And I say, "Well, when he comes home he'll start a fight and then your mom and dad'll get pissed," and Mike says fine. And he's acting really weird, and so I say I'm going to go and I go walking in the snow, but now everyone's been out and there's less and less places where I can leave fresh footprints and break a smooth surface. So then I go home and draw cyborgs.

Later, in the summer, Mike and I are at the pool. My dad dropped us off and on the way there was an Eagles song on the radio, where the singer said, "They had one thing in common, they were good in bed . . . ," which didn't make sense to me. And my dad laughed and said, "There's things you don't understand yet."

Mike's mom told him Mrs. Jeskyne is getting divorced from her husband.

"Some of the water in this pool was probably part of our snow fort," says Mike. But we're playing Shark Hunters now, and I don't understand what he's trying to say until much later in my life.

FULL DISCLOSURE

Stuff I did on the Internet while writing this chapter:

➤ Downloaded Bill Withers's *Just as I Am* from iTunes
➤ Watched three pwnage compilations on YouTube

Prelude to
"The Song of Ulvaak"

Dungeons and Dragons was the game I played. All through middle school and the first couple years of high school—until the possibility of sex hove into view. Before that, sex seemed like something for tall people who could run fast.

And here's how you played Dungeons and Dragons:

You got a sheet of paper. You got a pencil. You got three six-sided dice. On the sheet of paper you wrote, in a list, these six attributes: strength, intelligence, wisdom, constitution, dexterity, and charisma.

Got it?

You picked up the three dice, and you rolled 'em six times. One throw of the three dice for each attribute. Eighteen was the highest. Three was the lowest.

These six attribute scores became your "character." How strong, smart, wise, healthy, quick, and good-looking you were was all based on the roll of three dice.

Then you chose a race. And not black or white. An actual genus—human, dwarf, elf, halfling, half elf. Each race had advantages and liabilities. Dwarves were super-healthy and resistant to poisons. They were also ugly. Elves were more intelligent and graceful but were fragile. Halflings were small but quick and quiet.

I wonder if people realize how, simultaneously, Dungeons and Dragons was wildly progressive and archaic. Human beings were no longer black and white, male and female. We were all one, sharing the world, equal against the elves and halflings.

Of course, dwarves weren't human.

Then you chose a "class." That'd be your profession. Fighter, wizard, priest, or thief. There were subclasses—illusionist for wizards, ranger for fighters, for example.

Your attributes and your race determined what would be the perfect profession for your character. Dwarves made sturdy fighters but were clumsy with magic. Halflings made excellent thieves. Elves were the best magic users. Humans could pretty much do anything. Dungeons and Dragons was very egalitarian when it came to the human race. And seriously—what's with those sissy elves? Am I right?

An 18 strength meant you were a nigh-indestructible bruiser, able to bend bars, lift gates, and twist the head off of any foe who dared stand against you. An 18 intelligence meant that, as a wizard, you could memorize more spells, speak more languages, perhaps identify artifacts. An 18 dexterity made for a thief who could pick pockets and locks, climb walls, and backstab like a wicked finger of darkness.

One of your friends acted as Dungeon Master—he'd

design the adventure and stock a subterranean keep with fabulous wealth, powerful magical items, and deadly monsters guarding them. You and your other friends—and their characters—would venture into an imaginary hole in the crust of a pretend world and defeat fantasy beasts to gain possession of unspendable gold, jewels, and gems, as well as claim the right to wield magic rings, enchanted swords, blessed armor and artifacts, and scrolls that, when read, unleashed wonders that could change reality.

None of it changed *our* reality, of course. But winning a fantasy baseball league doesn't prevent you from having to go back to your stultifying tech job Monday morning, and there's no VIP champagne celebration waiting for you at the end of a fantasy Super Bowl. If the victories we create in our heads were let loose on reality, the world we know would drown in blazing happiness.

And that was Dungeons and Dragons. Six years of my young life. Roll abilities, pick a race, pick a profession, fight monsters, gain glory. All on paper, chronicled in graphite lead.

There were, of course, endless variations on this theme. I'm giving you the basics. This is how I was first introduced to the game, and despite a brief flirtation with an adult group of players in my late thirties—perhaps the most gentle, sedentary midlife crisis ever on record—this is how I remember it. You were supposed to "play" your character—a fighter who wasn't too smart and was prone to walking into danger; a thief who might not be very honest and loyal; a priest who, though able to heal and banish the undead, might come into conflict with the edicts of his god. But it really came down to a casino-like game of numbers—your attributes and skills against any monsters you might encounter.

You rolled those dice one last time to determine your hit points—the amount of damage you could take before you were dead. The monsters had their own hit points. And when you met, your axe or sword or lightning-bolt spell dealt out so much damage, and you absorbed so much damage from the swipe of a goblin's mace, the touch of a ghoul, or the breath of a dragon. You rolled more dice (a meteorlike twenty-sided die to determine if you'd scored a hit, an eight- or ten-sided die to determine damage) and your fate was decided by which side faced up when the dice came to rest. Gamblers at three A.M. live on the internal rush and collapse that come from the flip of a card, a ball falling into a slot, dice resting on felt. My friends and I, in basements and kitchens and in the cafeteria of Seneca Ridge Middle School on a Wednesday afternoon, rolled dice and heard, in our heads, the sound of orc skulls being split—or, oftentimes, the gurgling groan of our mighty fighter falling on the blood-soaked stones of a mossy crypt, ten feet away from a pile of gold and vorpal sword.

People committed suicide because of Dungeons and Dragons. Or plotted to kill one another. These were exceptions that proved the rule—Dungeons and Dragons was harmless fun (unless you counted all the snacks and soda poured into developing youngsters who were aggressively immobile). Someone twisted enough to take a game of paper, pencils, and pretend to a terminal extreme would have found a reason to end their life or deal out death in a *Family Circus* comic. Or the Bible.

Still, I wonder about all my past characters—Raphael the Thief, Delgath the Sorcerer, and Stumphammer, my profane, drunken dwarf warrior.

And most of all Ulvaak, the half-orc assassin (with his sentient sword, Bloodgusher—no, really). This was the last "character" I played before the gun of hormones fired me headlong into forever pursuing sex, and it shows.

Ulvaak was strength and violence incarnate. I was so addled with confusion, loneliness, and lust that I was in danger of falling out of the class-clown clique I normally hung with. Reciting Monty Python bits, paraphrasing *Saturday Night Live* sketches, trying to make Richard Pryor and George Carlin routines fit our everyday conversations—only now, puberty was a bag of cement lashed to my ankle. At least conversationally. Everything I thought and said now had this burning undercurrent of "How's this going to get me laid?" And wit can't have an agenda. So I clammed up, and I spent the summer between sophomore and junior years swimming, lifting weights, eating salad and fish, and clumsily trying to reroll the sorry stats I'd been given at birth.

So Ulvaak became my proxy during my clamp-jawed sophomore year. But he never made it past that summer.

18 Strength. He could punch through walls if I wanted him to. I all but bullied my Dungeon Master into giving him Gauntlets of Hill Giant Strength, upping his Strength stat to 19.

18 Constitution. He could take the sting of a cockatrice

tail, endure the deadly vapors of a green dragon's breath, or absorb a stab from one of his own envenomed daggers (worn in bandoliers across his blast-furnace chest) and shrug it off like a mild cold.

18 Dexterity. Fast—two-handed attacks, thrown knives always finding their mark, dodging an enemy's blows like an oiled serpent.

I fudged some of these rolls, by the way . . .

And, finally—*3* Charisma.

Three.

Repellent. Frightening. Not only did I conceive of Ulvaak as physically ugly—eyes crookedly set, a sneering maw full of gray teeth, horribly scarred from a slime monster attack—but also obnoxious and unpleasant. Cruel jokes, quick to anger, slow to calm—he was comfortable being everything that, in life, I wished I wasn't. Even at my politest, with my braces and cystic acne and snowman torso, no one wanted anything to do with me. So I created a fantasy character who had the strength, speed, and guts to back up every awkward remark I spent my days apologizing for. My comfort during the loneliest days of my adolescence was happy nihilism, which carried an ebony sword.

I left the hideous, confident bastard on a demon-fueled plane of existence. I remember it exactly—me and three other friends at our fourth friend's house. In the dining room. Sitting around the table—paper, pencils, dice, and lead figures to represent our characters.

The Dungeon Master had taken my figure off the table, to the side, to represent how he'd gone through a hell portal to a different plane of existence, where the sky was roiling blood and the ground was the scabbed-over corpse of a dead god. Ulvaak stood, in dragon-hide armor and a tattered cloak, holding Bloodgusher one-handed. The demon who ruled this hell plane—I forget his name—parlayed with Ulvaak, offering to send him back to the material plane of existence if he'd act as the demon's messenger and assassin.

Ulvaak served no man, monster, or demon. Knowing that slaying the demon lord would, in effect, destroy the hell plane he now stood on (it being a manifestation of the demon's ambition and avarice), he slung Bloodgusher like a burning shard from a graveyard explosion. It sliced the demon from shoulder to belly, and Ulvaak, the Black Blade of Gamotia, laughed as nameless damnation disintegrated beneath him and a sky of blood swallowed him whole.

Then I went to a pool party—the first one I was skinny enough to swim at without my shirt. I made out with a girl, and the curve of her hip and the soft jut of shoulder blades in a bikini forever trumped the imagined sensation of a sword pommel or spell book.

Sorry, Ulvaak. Will an epic poem make up for it?

The Song of Ulvaak

With a poisoned blade and a list of names
I stabbed and slashed and made my fame
For gold, I took lives free of blame
In the city of Gamotia

Gamotia! Teeming, dreaming jewel
Streets alive and quick and cruel
Fighter, warlock, priest, and fool
Could scheme for gold and glory

Each of us born, three dice thrown
Our strength, our brains, our fates alone
The sky gods chose our path—unknown
To even them, our story

Ringed with dungeons, breathing hell
Filled with weapon, wealth, and spell
And few who ventured lived to tell
But those who did—lived well

My sword was keen, my armor thick
No fighter's thrust or wizard's trick
Or curse from priest, or thieving pick
Could pierce my heart of stone

So off one day I rode and rode
Into a dungeon's maw I strode
Some beast to worry, bait, and goad
Then kill, to claim a bounty

Then down a crooked hallway crept
Across a spiked canyon leapt
Into a chamber, phantom-swept
There sat my newest prey

A hissing demon made of bone
A rotted tunic, eyes that shone
Regal, sat on silver throne
A zombie king, I reckoned

It made no difference—I'd been paid
A killer's contract had been made
This ghoul's head, severed, would be laid
On my retainer's table

Then up he sprang and drew a scroll
And with a voice dry-dark as coal
Began a chant that pierced my soul
And froze me where I stood

I wore two rings—one carved from jade
And one of mithril—Elvish made
The first one caused all magic to fade
The second made me swift

Not swift enough, or so it seemed
The ghoul's eyes, sockets, yet still gleamed
And then drew close, and grave mist steamed
Out of his hinge-y jaw

"Your contract's null, yet you will live
I'm not the one your death to give
That fate awaits—but, like a sieve,
Your time is running short."

He said, "There's worlds above our own
We are but fancies, proxies thrown
Into a dream—not flesh and bone
We are but dice and paper."

I'd long since learned—ignore the dead
The eldritch legions deal in dread
And riddles, hexes, teasing, led
The foolish to their doom

But he'd touched something long suspected
And my confidence infected
Weakened, shook—his words projected
Louder in that room

"We're hero figures for the weak
Who aren't yet confident to speak
To girls, or claim the life they seek,"
The ghoul said with a sigh

"And so we wade through blood and gore
Claim a treasure, bed a whore
Accomplish deeds beyond a door
The 'gods' have not yet opened."

Then all his matter turned to dust
Away he flew upon a gust
Of death-fed wind; my body-rust
Was, all at once, no more

Back in Gamotia, suddenly
(Or had it always bothered me?)
I sensed a subtle falsity
In every face I spied

Their skills and defects, will and wit
Seemed paper-thin and counterfeit
Their fates the same and long pre-writ
Off in some far-off sky

The sky! I noticed, seemed to be
Of crumpled foolscap, torn—and me
No longer was I a killer free
To guide my own life's path

I sensed, somewhere outside the land,
A soft and inexperienced hand
That knew no steel and claimed no land
Had brought me into being

And so decided, in a flash
I'd not be tossed away like trash
My sword would rend and gnaw and lash
Against a pudgy god

[At this point "The Song of Ulvaak" suddenly stops and
is replaced by the transcribed lyrics of Phil Collins's "One
More Night," followed by an embarrassing and desperate love note.]

On a Street
in New Orleans

71

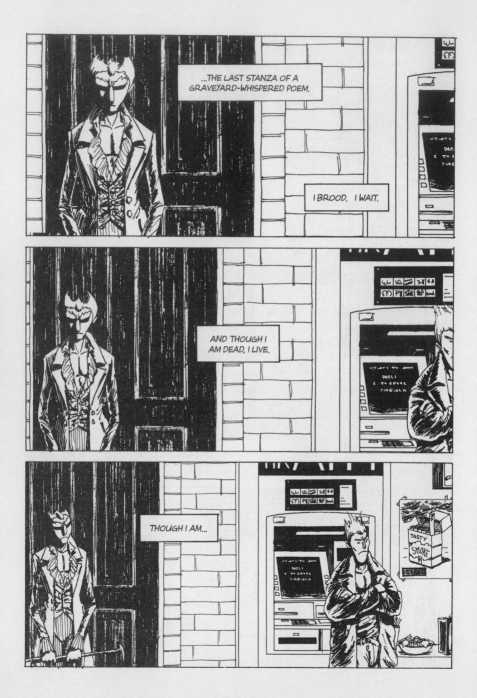

72

74

78

Peter Runfola

My uncle Pete was insane.

I know there was a proper medical term, a specific *diagnosis,* for what he had. A sort of schizophrenia or something. But that knowledge died with my grandfather, who took care of Pete for most of his sixty or so years.* Pete died a few years before Grandfather, which was just as well. Grandpa Runfola was attuned to Pete's moods and rhythms. He could fend off an angry spell, quell daylight demons, and guide Pete through foggy fugues instinctively. They lived together—a divorcée and his huge, shaggy, bachelor son, in College Park, Maryland. Their house was just blocks away from the house that Pete, his two brothers and one sister (my mom), and, at the time, my still-married grandfather and grandmother grew up in.

Well, no . . . *not* my grandfather and grandmother. They didn't grow up in that house or anywhere, really. My grandfather and grandmother grew up, separately, elsewhere. They collided in their youth, sent four kids flying into the world, and then continued on without each

*Didn't even cross my mind to write "sixty-odd."

79

other. Except for Thanksgiving and Christmas, which were unspoken rally points in their solitary lives, when they'd get together with their four kids at either our house, one of the uncles', or—best of all, in my opinion—at Grandpa Runfola's. Other than that, it was a condo in Chevy Chase for Grandma and the little house in College Park for Grandpa and Uncle Pete.

Grandpa's house in College Park was my favorite. So much better than Grandma's sterile Chevy Chase condo. At the condo, after dinner had been consumed, the adults were drawn in two directions. The men coalesced around sports on a television and short, bumblebee bursts of travel to the wet bar. The women sat with them and gossiped about work, kids, and celebrities. It was the first musical mash-up I can remember hearing—the headlong pulse of a football game, with the driving drone of the announcer's voice and the occasional whoop and bark of adults praising or condemning this or that godDAMN that or yyyyEEEEESSSS or AWWWWwwww (shit). And then, laid over this, like gulls over a noisy summer beach of dropped hot dog bits and popcorn kernels, the women, who can't beLIEVE how STUpid this one at work is or HORRible this one kid on the block is or HOW she can stand to be photographed when she's so FAAAAAAT? A high treble of lip-smacking snark over the drum and bass of sports.

My brother loved sports. I couldn't believe anyone could follow any conflict that didn't involve lasers, robots, or magic rings.

I'd go out on the balcony and swoop up the crusty

snow on the railings and drop it far far far into the empty courtyard.

Uncle Pete would join me out there on the icy balcony. Not that he hated sports or even company. I assumed, at the time, he was the only other person who understood the inherent awesomeness of shattering ice sheets and *plaaaap*ing balls of soft snow on concrete, which looked, from that perspective, like spells or evil presences smashing against the gray wall of reality, not getting through.

What I didn't know was that Pete already had a hundred songs and voices and movies and gods in his head, chattering and flirting and arguing in an eternal overlit salon. It probably seemed rude, to him, to subject a group of job-holding, tax-paying, child-raising adults to such a cosmic and otherworldly standard. You wouldn't let Barney Fife go up against the Man with No Name or the Magnificent Seven, would you?

We stood on the balcony, Uncle Pete and I. My breath came out in a clean fog in the winter air and he exhaled an empty gray exhaust from the cigarettes he chain-smoked. Pete hadn't started growing his mad-Russian-priest beard. He wore thick horn-rimmed glasses. He had a square, clean-shaven face that looked like any number of people you'd see in the background of an early-fifties group photo of a searching party.

"Think you could hit those ravens with your snow bombs?" he asked, pointing down to a huddle of black birds on a branch two stories beneath us.

"I could, but it'd be mean."

"They'd bomb *you* if they could. That's what they're

talking about now," he said, going back inside for another handful of the endless peanuts he used to wash down his cigarettes. I looked back down at the ravens, and as if they felt my gaze, they huddled together closer.

I thought Pete was the coolest person in the world.

And he lived in the coolest house ever. A little suburban bungalow, perched on a corner off the highway, with this weird backyard that swooped and rose, abutting other backyards that swooped and rose. Standing on the back porch, you looked out onto a stormy ocean of grass, flash-frozen at its angriest moment. Whoever designed College Park, Maryland, must have been quietly terrified of the landscape and left it untouched, as if the confused, dark, and ancient forces that carved the surface had signed it with an exclamation point.*

---

*The house that Pete and my mother and their siblings grew up in— their *original* house, a few blocks over, and not the one Pete and Grandpa moved to—was down the street from where the kid who inspired *The Exorcist* lived. Pete and my mother would talk about it obliquely, and they'd never go into detail. But Pete's details, scant as my mother's, were vivid. "You'd walk by the place and you could kind of hear that someone was screaming in the upstairs bedroom, but there'd also be traffic and noises and they kept the window shut, so you'd also think maybe you were hearing things," said Pete. I'd wonder—how young was he when his schizophrenia began to blossom and the volume knob began to crank toward the red? Was this kid's demonic yowling somehow mixed with whatever unreliable memories Pete viewed through the thicket of his madness?

And then, in the next sentence, Pete would lay in a more prosaic—and, by virtue of its blandness, more valuable—detail: "Father Bowdern went away for a few months with this kid, somewhere in the Midwest, and they say they cured him." And then the thicket would close in again: "But when Father Bowdern came back, me and the other altar boys could tell he wasn't Father Bowdern anymore." And then one final, comforting frosting flower of reality: "Anyway, the house is gone now. They put a gazebo up in its place. You and your brother used to walk down there all the time when you were little."

* * *

"Nevermore," said Pete, slamming himself down in the chair next to mine at the little kitchen table.

I was laughing. He said "nevermore" in this weird, TV-horror-movie-host voice, and he bugged his eyes out.

He had a thick book in front of him, and one of his thumbs was marking a page.

"Quoth the Raven . . . ," said Pete. And then, fumbling the book open, he started from the beginning of Edgar Allan Poe's "The Raven."

That was my first encounter with Poe—being read "The Raven," without preamble, introduction, or context, by my insane uncle in a tiny kitchen in College Park. And he read it like a little kid discovering it—making a poem about adult regret and loneliness seem like the greatest thing to a kid who thought coolness acted like the Fonz, sounded like Kiss, and rode a motorcycle like Evel Knievel.

My world was fun, but I always suspected there was more. Vampires in a room shuttered against California sunshine. A snow fort melted into the water that we swam in at the community pool in summer. Heroes and villains created at the flick of a pencil tip or in the tumblings of a handful of dice. My parents could drive us to Washington, DC, to get freeze-dried ice cream at the Air and Space Museum or ride the rides at Kings Dominion, or take us to movies. They could drop me off at an airport to take a plane to visit my other grandparents, out in the Arizona desert. Still, the world felt *bounded*. Uncle Pete was the first one ever to heave open the gates that sealed ancient pages and make me suspect there were worlds within and without the world I was in. That there were worlds outside of the *time* I was living in. All of this he carried against his will, in his head. But unlike the other adults, with their resentments and their anxiousness or anger, he seemed eternally, uncontrollably *entertained*. I really envied him.

And then, before I knew it was happening, Pete became a living totem for everything I wanted to avoid in my life.

I'm sitting here writing this and I can't track the exact change. But it happened. I grew into my teens and I grew afraid of awkwardness. Pete grew out his beard like he was God's cartoon and retreated farther and farther back into the thicket. And, more than anyone in my family and *way* more than anyone I've ever met or would become myself, he was comfortable and happy being quietly, anti-socially batshit crazy.

Occasionally visiting Pete and Grandpa in my teen years forever soured me on the "holy fool" portrayals of the insane and eccentric in films. You know the ones I'm talking about—pale and unshaven, but always rakishly so, with a clowny glint of kooky wisdom in their eyes and an elliptical way of muttering hip-shot revelations the rest of us are ignoring, unaware of, or dancing around like some monstrous flame. Who can brave the shaman heat of the truth? Why, kooky Aunt Lottie, who wears earrings she made from toothbrushes and names all the squirrels!

I'd be brooding about some teenage slight I'd conflated in my teenage mind, and Pete'd come into the kitchen.

"You all right?"

I'd say, "Sort of."

Here's Pete's chance to Sort It All Out: "That old lady in the commercial for the Clapper? Someone should clap her in her face."

No help.

I began thinking of life—a *real* life—being about movement and travel and awareness. Or, at least, I thought awareness came from seeing the world, experiencing it. I still think that.

And that's where Pete and I parted ways, slowly and then all of a sudden.

As the thicket closed its final branches around Pete's mind, he built a soundproof chamber in broad daylight. Out on the front porch of the little College Park house, he'd sit in his chair, sunup to sundown (and, truth be told, far beyond the darkness), and listen to the Washington, DC, oldies station. They'd still take requests and, over the years, Pete became a minor celebrity, at least among the six-strong crew of deejays who regularly took his calls for requests—the Elegants' "Little Star" was an abiding favorite. When winter came he ran an extension cord from inside the house to a heating pad he'd sit on, baking his body like a mound of dough inside the clay oven of his winter parka.

And coffee. Endless cups of coffee. From the same chewed and bruised Styrofoam cup from the 7-Eleven down the street. He'd bring it back, use it until the edges of the bottom literally dissolved. Only then would he deign to grab a new one from next to the coffeepot. He would use a cup until it no longer existed as a cup.

And there he'd sit. He was still lucid, and relatively young, but I could imagine his features blurring and sliding beneath the beard. I could imagine his body sagging and spreading and creaking under the parka in winter and under his sail-like, oversized cotton shirts in the summer. Who knows what his mind was doing, raging and humming and slowing to a white crawl and then lurching forward in blue-hot bursts of mixed sound, memory, and random images. There was nothing in the eyes to tell you. When he spoke it still related, pretty lucidly, to whatever or whomever was in front of him. If there were poison, dragons, or ghosts behind his greetings or good-byes, I never saw it. I just saw my uncle Pete, sitting in place, and knew that wasn't how I wanted to live my life. I suspected, around the time I graduated college, that we're all versions of targets, fired at by indifferent events. If that was the case, then I wanted to be a moving target.

What sealed my final, silent drifting away from Uncle Pete was a Christmas when we visited the College Park house. I was in the early stages of realizing I wanted to move to San Francisco, to get serious about being a comedian. When you're beginning to suspect you might be leaving a place, you become hypersensitive to it, as if your mind is subconsciously stocking itself with smells, sounds, sights, and tactile sensations of a place you'll no longer see every day.

So that Christmas, the one before I headed west, was a feast even before I sat down at the table. I can vividly remember the smell of the fireplace in my grandfather's basement, the feel of the fabric on his couch. Snow was visible, falling, through the big glass doors in the back of the living room. And I remember how it made the white winter light ripple like seawater. I couldn't summon the illusion of the house rising through the air, but I tried. And I can taste every bit of that Thanksgiving-by-way-of-working-class-Italian-cuisine dinner. The turkey, with a side of macaroni and peas. The rolls and roasted peppers. And the cheap jug wine, so sweet against the green-bean-and-onion casserole.

And I couldn't take my eyes off Pete. He ate dinner like he always did, in three or four huge, whoofing bites, before heading back out front to his cone of warmth, his coffee, his cigarettes, and ghostly tunes piping from his little transistor radio. And, most important, to whatever thoughts drowned out the voices of his own family saying "hello" and "happy holidays."

I watched him because I couldn't believe that could be anyone's comfortable horizon. A tiny porch on a dark corner near a highway. We lucked out living on a planet made thrilling by billions of years of chance, catastrophe, miracles, and disaster, and he'd rejected it. You're offered the world every morning when you open your eyes. I was beginning to see Pete as a representative of all the people who shut that out, through cynicism, religion, fear, greed, or ritual.

We were on our way home. My dad realized he needed to stop in the 7-Eleven for something. I went in with him.

Another man was asking the clerk for directions, farther up the road from where we'd come.

The clerk said, "Well, you keep heading back the way you were, right?"

"Okay," said the man.

"And you'll get to a corner. 'Bout a mile up?"

"Yeah."

"And there's this house, and there's going to be a fat guy with a huge beard sitting out front listening to the radio. That's where you take your right."

Pete had become a landmark.

Pete died a few years after I'd moved to LA. The chain-smoking, junk food, and immobility had finally gotten their message through to the rest of his body, and it quietly shut down.

"Pete had his own little world there, you know?" said my mom over the phone.

At this point in my life, I'd traveled over a fourth of the planet. I'd been to little towns and marveled at some random person—maybe a cineaste who visited the same little movie theater in Prague every night, or a craggy bar denizen in Dublin who inhabited the same stool, or even the crazies in Los Angeles, dancing shirtless on the same stretch of sidewalk, holding up signs for the disinterested commuters to honk at.

I was still hungry to travel and move and create and connect—and I always will be—but I've got to admit something.

There's a little bit of Pete in me. There always was, and there always will be. Maybe it'll grow stronger as I grow older, maybe not. But it's there. I still don't agree with spending a life the way Pete did, but I understand it and respect it. Who knows how many lives have been saved and villains vanquished by those who sat still?

Will anything we do last? No. I just read a quote by Sir David Rees: "Most educated people are aware that we are the outcome of nearly 4 billion years of Darwinian selection, but many tend to think that humans are somehow the culmination. Our sun, however, is less than halfway through its lifespan. It will not be humans who watch the sun's demise, 6 billion years from now. Any creatures that exist will be as different from us as we are from bacteria or amoeba."

On the day Pete died, someone left a fresh cup of coffee on his empty seat in front of the house in College Park. A nod from a fellow human who, like Pete, had started out as cosmic matter, shared with the stars above him, in an explosion eons ago.

And, long before Pete disintegrated out of this world, he'd become a happy ghost in his own heat-pad heaven—a paradise of tobacco, caffeine, and "Little Star."

FULL DISCLOSURE

Stuff I did on the Internet while writing this chapter:

➤ Played a game called Treasure Seas, Inc., while listening to the *In Our Time* podcast
➤ Deleted my MySpace inbox and then deleted my MySpace trash
➤ Looked at photos of search parties from the fifties

Wines by the Glass

WHITES BY THE GLASS

MUSTARD TIPTOE VINEYARDS   FRESNO

"THE SENSITIVE TEEN" CHARDONNAY $8

Overprotected, easily frightened white first-growth grapes with hints of butterflies, honeysuckle, and tears. A dramatic first palate with a fey, whiney finish. Great with fish, steamed veggies, or Livingston Taylor music.

TAMBY   WILLAMETTE VALLEY

"HEATHAZE" PINOT GRIGIO $10

Asphalt, licorice, and tobacco over a confused bed of summer squash. A mouse died in one of the barrels. Is that where your glass came from?

THREE DOTS FADING   SOMEWHERE IN A
                                  MIDNIGHT DESERT

"OBSCURA" CHENIN BLANC $14

A finger tracing a friend's demise in a pile of spilled sugar on a mahogany table. Cherries. Black pepper winking at a werewolf who just took the wrong contract. An idea hiding in a shoe. The swordsman! A winter morning! No percentage in kittens.

PRECIOUS OBJECT VILLA

"UNATTAINABLE" RIESLING   VARIABLE

Angel sweat strained through diamond mesh into a platinum tureen hammered smooth by three former presidents and the current pope. Stored in an oak barrel made from the Tree of Life, bottled by billionaires, and poured into your glass by a scientist or poet. And Bob Dylan will personally watch you drink it. Although, now that we think of it, we'd rather you weren't seen imbibing this wine. No, choose something else. No. Something else. Are you still talking?

REDS BY THE GLASS

FRED LUDD   GARY, INDIANA

"DRINKABLE" MERLOT $2

A bunch of grapes, and they're smooshed, and then they get kind of rotten, and we drain off the alcohol part and that's the part you drink and then you're drunk. Are you going to finish that burger?

COLLEGE TOWN VINEYARDS

"FRESHMAN AT THANKSGIVING" PINOT NOIR　　$11

A Nietzschean blend of arrogant pinot grapes, half-informed with an amusing smugness. Fermented in stainless steel vats, formed from iron ore mined by exploited workers in Guatemala, whom our government uses as drug mules to fund a shadow war that's gone unreported for more than fifty years. Great when paired with Gang of Four or Fugazi CDs, southern Hunan cuisine (not the northern provinces, which are so fucking mainstream I want to puke), and ironic T-shirts.

CRACKING CROW HILL

AUSTRALIAN SHIRAZ　　$9

A binky wosgow of keezy plinkers, hoop-daddied for a 'dillo's wink and flappled in a pongo. Hints of sweet bashie, roasted wopabaggle, and frum-dipped mollys. A right chickamoo!

FINZULLI FAMILY　　PIEDMONT, ITALY

NEBBIOLO　　$12

Made from the finest, richest freisa grapes, stolen during the late October fogs in the Langhe region, from the Spezzanio family. Their oldest son, Nino, tried to stop our soldiers, but we cut the bastard down with our shotguns and sent the ears back to his mother, who had a knife slid between our cousin Lalo's ribs during the Feast of the Virgin last spring.

SPARKLING WINES

CHEBORNEK VLAD	ROMANIA
VIN SPUMOS	$14

Is bubbles! For faggots!

SPEZZANIO FAMILY	PIEDMONT, ITALY
PROSECCO	$15

Nino! Oh God, Neeeeeee-no!

DESSERT WINES

MEINGUTENFUHRER ISSINWEIN GERMANY	$15

The whitest, purest grapes are separated from the darker, weaker ones (which are trucked off before the wine's final solution) and used to make a clean, strong strain of ice wine. A triumph of the will.

Zombie Spaceship Wasteland

Are you a Zombie, a Spaceship, or a Wasteland?

For my group of friends, after seeing *Star Wars* in 1977, around age eight, and then *Night of the Living Dead* and all the eighties slasher films once VCRs sprouted on top of our TVs, and *The Road Warrior* in 1981, the answer to that question decided our destinies.

I know there have been a thousand parsings of the pop subculture—comic books, video games, horror movies, heavy metal, science fiction, Dungeons and Dragons. There are hundreds more categories. They can be laid out in overlapping Venn diagrams—a tub full of lonely bubbles. Burnouts who are into heavy metal got there through Dungeons and Dragons, maybe some glam rock, probably horror movies. Hard-core comic book readers often became film snobs later in life (they spend their adolescence reading, essentially, storyboards). Even sports freaks*—with their endless, exotic game stats— overlapped into metal and, yeah, maybe comic books.

---

*Not to be confused with jocks or athletes—a distinction beautifully laid out by Sarah Vowell in *Take the Cannoli,* a book very much worth your time.

But for me, and my circle of high school friends, it came down to *Zombies, Spaceships,* or *Wastelands.* These were the three doors out of the Vestibule of Adolescence, and each opened onto a dark, echoing hallway. The corridors twisted and intertwined, like a DNA helix. Maybe those paths were a rough reflection of the DNA we were born with, which made us more likely to cherish and pursue one corridor over another.

I'm going to try to explain each of these categories (and will probably fail). And then I'll figure out where I came out, on the other end, once the cards were played. I think this chapter is more for me than for you.

Each of these categories represents differents aspects of a shared teen experience—not fully understanding how the world works, socially or economically. The early out-casts—like me—were late to sex and careers. If we did find a vocation, it usually involved drawing or writing or *something* creative—work that's done in the home, and usually alone. The real-world experience we're going to need, as writers or artists or filmmakers, will come later, when we actually have to get a real job to support what-ever creative thing we're hoping to do.

So until then, anything we create has to involve *sim-plifying, leaving,* or *destroying* the world we're living in.

Zombies simplify. They don't understand the world any better than Spaceships or Wastelands, but they sure like the houses and highways. Every zombie story is fundamentally about a breakdown of order, with the infrastructure intact. That infrastructure might be on fire, yes. And it's great fun to crash a bus through a department store window as the driver finds himself torn to shreds by the suddenly zombified passengers. But the world, appearance-wise, survives. It might eventually become a wasteland (more advanced Zombies begin their stories far in the future, where the world is already a wasteland), but for now, it's a microcosm of archetypes, fighting for survival against the undead hordes. Usually this small group is made up of the archetypes that the teen has met thus far into his short existence—the Hero, the Unattainable Hottie, the Loudmouth Douchebag, and the Brainiac Who Knows What's Going On. Consistent with an awkward teen's roiling sense of vengeance and self-hatred, it's usually only the Loudmouth Douchebag and the Brainiac who get killed.

Usually, but not often. Since Zombies follow their path into horror, Goth, slasher films, some punk rock, and most metal, Zombies tend to be the most nihilistic of the three. Thus, most zombie movies—including the classic *Night of the Living Dead*—end with every single character dead.

A friend of mine from high school—more of a passing acquaintance, now that I think of it—was a hard-core zombie before he even knew it. He had an unshakable love for the awkward and outcast and a quiet, final disgust with the slick and false. And he divided everyone into one of these two categories, with maybe three subsets for each (Physically Awkward, Mentally Awkward, Sports Slick, Republican Slick—you get the idea).

Years later, when I'd moved to L.A., he sent me a zombie script he'd written. Not a bad effort. Not a great one.

At one point in the script, one of the characters knocks a zombie off of a boat. The zombie struggles for a moment, trying to stay afloat, and then sinks.

I asked him, innocently, "It never occurred to me—would a zombie care if it were underwater or not? They don't breathe. Would they even know?"

This was his terse answer: "For your information, zombies can live underwater, *they just don't like it.*"

He was a Zombie who'd long ago taken a zombie-eyed view of the world. You see them everywhere—rolling their eyes outside a rock club at how lame the band was, shaking their heads over a newspaper in a coffeeshop, resentful under office lighting. Zombies can't believe the energy we waste on nonfood pursuits.

Night of the Living Dead (and most zombie films) is about *Zombies* who are in the process of turning the world into a *Wasteland,* and who've been brought back to life by radiation on a crashed *Spaceship*.

Spaceships leave. No surviving infrastructure for them. No Earth, period. *That* would still involve people.

Better to not only leave the world, but to create a new one and decide how the creatures (or human-looking aliens) act. Often, the alien planet they populate is a glorified wasteland. But even in that wasteland, Spaceships figure it's easier for them to build a world and know its history or, better yet, choose the limited customs and rituals that fit the story. Every Spaceship kid I knew growing up now works in computers. They got there through

New Wave, post-punk, video games, and science fiction. Why bother reading subtle facial cues and emotional signals when there's a vast (yet finite) map of a motherboard to tinker with?

But, being Spaceships, they describe in the most loving detail the spaceships that zoom between worlds. "Laser cannons" take the place of conversation, "deflector shields" are emotional nuance, and "warp drive" is story exposition. The opening shot of *Star Wars,* with the sleek rebel ship and then the massive Imperial Star Destroyer, barreling across the screen like the pan across a party in an Altman film, permanently doomed a generation of Spaceships to their insular, slightly muted lives. Spaceships have the hallway with the most gravity, firmly pulling its victims down a cool tunnel of romantic vacuum. In their bodies, skulls, and spirits, a chunk of my peers became Spaceships, skimming over the surface of the world, maneuvering through their own lives. Deflector shields up.

Spaceships are the ones most likely to get married and have kids. They treat their houses like spaceships that have landed on earth, and their spouses and kids like crew members. Which makes them pretty good parents—they've always got emergency kits, lists of most-used numbers, backup supplies of ointment, painkillers, and bottled water. The two guys I spent my youth building Lego spaceships with are two of the greatest dads I've ever known—a good captain knows how to treat his crew.

Darth Vader is, essentially, a *Zombie*, born in a *Wasteland,* who works on a *Spaceship*.

* * *

Wastelands destroy. They're confused but fascinated by the world. So the idea of zooming off in a self-contained spaceship, no matter how lovingly described or sensually evoked,* smacks of retreat. But the blandness of the world we've built—a lot of Wastelands come from the suburbs—frustrates and frightens them as much as the coldness of space. Aliens would bring wonder, and zombies bring the surviving humans together—Wastelands aren't comfortable with either of those ideas.

The solution? Wasteland. Post-nuke, post–meteor strike, or simply a million years into the future—that's the perfect environment for the Wasteland's imagination to gallop through. The wasteland is inhabited by people or, for variety, mutants. At least mutants are outgrowths of humans. Mutants—the main inhabitants of postapocalyptic environments—are more familiar. Variations of the human species grown amok—isn't that how some teenage outcasts already feel? Mutants bring comfort. You don't have to figure out alien biology or exotic, inhuman cultures or religions. At the most, mutants will have weird mental powers or practice cannibalism. The heroes are unmutated humans, wandering across deserts (always, weirdly, wearing leather or tattered overcoats—suburban teens are accustomed to air-conditioning, so it's not until they're older that they learn the importance of fab-

---

*The spaceship in *Battle Beyond the Stars* has huge breasts and a woman's voice!

rics that breathe) and carrying what they need. Wastelands are great at stocking belt pouches, backpacks, and
pockets. At any time, Wastelands suspect they're going to
need to grab whatever's at hand and head for the horizon.

Wastelands are almost always swallowed up by punk
rock and science fiction. They're also the most likely to
keep journals and usually the first to get menial jobs. The
Wasteland tarot card should come with a pay stub.

Weirdly, Wastelands are the most hopeful and sentimen-
tal of the bunch. Because even though they've destroyed
the world as we know it, they conceive of stories in which
a core of humanity—either in actual numbers of survivors
or in the conscience of a lone hero—survives and endures.
Wastelands, in college, love Beckett.

The monster in *Alien* was discovered on a *Spaceship* that
had crashed in a *Wasteland,* and reproduced by temporarily turning its victims into alien-incubating *Zombies.*

Leatherface, Michael Myers, Jason Voorhees, Pinhead,
and Freddy Krueger are, essentially, *Zombies* who want
to turn our world into a *Wasteland.* Jason and Pinhead
each, at one point, end up on a *Spaceship.*

The *Matrix* films are about a hero, Neo, who doesn't
realize he's a *Zombie,* and also doesn't realize he's living in a *Wasteland,* until he's awoken by Morpheus, who
de-zombifies Neo by bringing him on board a *Spaceship.*

* * *

Every teen outcast who pursues a creative career has, at its outset, either a Zombie, Spaceship, or Wasteland work of art in them.

Looking back on it now, I realize I'm a Wasteland. A lot of comedians are Wastelands—what is stand-up comedy except isolating specific parts of culture or humanity and holding them up against a stark, vast background to approach at an oblique angle and get laughs? Or, in a broader sense, pointing out how so much of what we perceive as culture and society is disposable waste? Plus, comedians have to work the Road. We wander the country, seeking outposts full of cheap booze, nachos, and audiences in order to ply our trade. I'm amazed we all don't wear sawed-off shotguns on our hips.

The Zombie, Spaceship, or Wasteland "work" is conceived of during the nadir of puberty—a grim, low-budget film about the undead; a vast space opera; or a final battle for civilization in a blasted wasteland, where the fate of mankind is decided by a shotgun blast or a crossbow.

Turns out I had two Wasteland works in me, and I wrote them both freshman year of high school. The first was called *The Shadow Dogs,* which I figured I'd publish in paperback, like a Stephen King novel.* It involved— I'm not kidding—a future where mutant dogs had taken

---

*Stephen King, who was the first person I ever read who could meld perfectly felt, mundane life with cosmic horror, later published the *Dark Tower* series, a huge Wasteland epic that tied together most of his novels, which take place in our "real" world. And I'm pretty sure he got the idea in high school. If he didn't, I would like him to lie about it to support my thesis. Thanks, Steve!

over. They were basically tall people with dog heads. The hero—I can't even remember his name—wandered the wasteland with a cool wrist gun and another sidearm that I basically swiped from *Blade Runner,* which I still think has one of the coolest movie guns.

Hey—why do the heroes always "wander" the wasteland? Wouldn't you at least have a plan to get somewhere with water or food before you started hoofing it? Even desert nomads don't "wander" around pell-mell, assuming they'll hit an oasis just before dropping dead of thirst. Is it the alliteration of it? "Wander the wasteland"? I guess "Take a well-thought-out, purposeful trek through the wasteland" lacks that movie-trailer punch.

Anyway, *The Shadow Dogs.* I spent the first eighty pages of the novel equipping my main character. I'm not kidding—he started with a bolt-action rifle and a knife, and then he killed some people and took enough canned food and other trinkets from them to trade for the wrist gun and *Blade Runner* gun. Once I realized I couldn't think of any cooler guns for him to acquire, I lost interest in the book.

The other one was called *Cholly Victor and the Wasteland Blues,* which I wrote in installments and planned to do as a massive graphic novel. Cholly Victor was a near-plotless library of everything I was obsessed with at the time—*The Road Warrior, El Topo, Eraserhead,* Richard Corben, nuclear fears, and spaghetti westerns. Holy God, was it a piece of crap. But I got it out of my system. It ends with my hero, Cholly, a shotgun-wielding wasteland scavenger, defeating a mutant, flayed-lamb robot warlord, and then continuing on down a piece of broken highway to the mythical "Westcoast."*

My own life didn't even come close to my defeating a robot warlord and setting out for Westcoast. In reality, I got sick of doing jokes in front of the zombies at the local comedy clubs. I moved to San Francisco. In a used Jetta, not a spaceship. And driving cross-country wasn't "wandering the wasteland," but Utah came close enough.

---

*Cormac McCarthy won the Pulitzer for *The Road*, about a father and son making their way for a mythical coast after an unnamed global cataclysm. But Cormac's hero didn't have a four-armed, bandolier-wearing mutant Kodiak bear sidekick, did he?

Chamomile Kitten
Greeting Cards

IT'S A BOY!

The "winged baby basket" drawing on this Chamomile Kitten™ greeting card was the secret sigil of the "dacianos," or "freak makers." These were Gypsy baby thieves who, at the behest of bored royalty, would kidnap low-born children and make them into freaks for the amusement of the prevailing royal court. They were grown in jars that splayed and warped their limbs or had their soft skulls gently pressed into squares; there was no limit to the myriad variations that could be wrought onto a developing human infant.

It's rumored that the dacianos lurk on the outskirts of society today, always ready to snatch a fresh, wriggling bundle of "merchandise" for use in secret, subterranean "freak theaters" to entertain bored celebrities after they endure protracted, soul-crushing events like Oscar, Emmy, and Tony award ceremonies.

Forever on the lookout for pregnant bellies, couples attending baby safety classes, or *anyone* purchasing a birth announcement card, the dacianos wait.

They wait.

We hope this Chamomile Kitten™ greeting card has helped spread the joy you feel welcoming your wee one to the world!

EASTER!

The playful "bunny and egg basket" illustration on this Chamomile Kitten™ greeting card is taken from a German book of children's holiday folklore.

According to the story "The Hare Who Went Forth with Unborn Chickens to Fatten the Children," the King of Rabbits was becoming worried about the world's dwindling rabbit population. Keep in mind this story was written in 1713, when a plate of boiled rabbit, sauerkraut, and dandelion tubers was the most prized "treat" among rural children.

The Chicken Emperor, gloating over the demise of the rabbits (the archenemies of chickens, at least according to the story), had decreed that his hens produce twice as many eggs so that the chicken populace could fill the soon-to-be-vacated niche the rabbits inhabited in the world.

But the King of Rabbits had a trick up his sleeve. Switching all the new chicken eggs with white stones, the rabbits boiled the unborn chickens in their shells and then painted the eggs bright colors. They left these brightly colored eggs, along with eggs made of chocolate, in festive baskets in the children's homes while they slept.

The visual association of bright colors and the taste of sweet chocolate, all in egg form, created an insatiable hunger for eggs in the children of the world. The story ends—like most German children's tales—with one animal cursing God and the horror at the heart of the universe, while another animal performs a happy, demonic murder dance under blue moonlight.

We hope this Chamomile Kitten™ greeting card helps you have a "hoppy" Easter!

ST. PATRICK'S DAY

The shamrock etching on this Chamomile Kitten™ greeting card was taken from the preinked outline of a tattoo. The tattoo was worn on the inner thigh of Fyn "Finn" McManus, a legendary brawler in early nineteenth-century New York. His capacity for alcohol, vomiting, and fisticuffs earned him the nickname "the Whiskey Abyss," and one of his favorite pastimes included "parading." "Parading" was his own pet name for drinking his age in ounces of whiskey, and then walking down the sidewalks, randomly punching and eructing on passersby. Several attempts by local constables to prohibit this practice proved unsuccessful, until an amiable foot patrolman—his name lost to history—hit upon a novel solution.

When McManus's customary pre-parading cry was

heard as he left whatever tavern or blind tiger he'd just completed his "age/ounce" ritual in (the cry being a variation of the phrase "*A-cummin there ta make soup bowls a' faces and fill 'em with chowder!*") the local police would spring into action.

Gently guided to the center of the street, McManus could land blows and launch effluvium at whatever "pedestrians" he perceived to be in his path—invariably, horses and the carriages they pulled.

McManus met his end on the balmy evening of May 2, 1912, when he mistook the Happy Cat Tooth Powder mascot painted on the front of an onrushing streetcar for a bartender who had recently refused him service. McManus charged and promptly disappeared in a spray of knuckles and vomit.

We hope this Chamomile Kitten™ greeting card helps you safely and soberly celebrate the "wearin o' the green"!

GRADUATION

The mortarboard-and-tassel flourish on this Chamomile Kitten™ greeting card is a fun optical illusion. While the image *appears* to, indeed, be the traditional headwear of the successful college graduate, it is actually an inverted and reversed "tunnel mouth" design. Designed by minimalist painter Skaate Inskviln in 1901, the tunnel mouth was, according to a self-published monograph, a "dream conception" of the entranceway to "a world that is a path."

The painting, called *The Road of Quench-less Striving*, was first shown at a small Swabian university in 1903. More than fifteen students, all on the verge of graduation, began experiencing insomnia, severe gastric distress, and bleeding pupils after viewing it. The painting has never been shown again.

However, one of the students who suffered eight months of insomnia wrote an opera shortly after being released from a sleep disorder clinic. Titled *I Have Spent Eight Years Learning from the Lives of People Who Truly Broke Free from the Strictures of Higher Education and Actually Made Their Lives What They Wanted While I Have Failed to Follow Their Example, Will Continue to Fail, and Will Die Unmourned, Confused, and Fat,* it was never performed.

Skaate Inskviln was bitten by a scorpion and died in a Tempe, Arizona, whorehouse in 1913.

We hope this Chamomile Kitten™ greeting card sets you off on the right foot on your path of success!

HALLOWEEN

The image on this Chamomile Kitten™ greeting card is from the frontispiece of Braeburn Vollrath's *The Howler at the Rim of Eternity,* first published by Arkham House in 1921. It is a subdued reproduction of the Aryan Idiot-Cannibal Fetish, carved into the litten arch of the Greblischtenmorgue and presumably destroyed after the building was firebombed at the end of World War II.

Vollrath, who died in the San Quentin gas chamber (he reportedly strapped himself in), said of the image, "Its gaze unlocked a room in my nightmares which should have remained closed." Shortly after publication of *The Howler,* Vollrath was arrested and confessed to the Cambridge Jawbone Murder Spree. Despite overwhelming evidence of a second killer, Vollrath famously repeated, "The face. The face in the stone and me alone." The late-seventies Finnish death-metal band Hastur used this quote as a refrain in their song "Howler."

Few, if any, copies of *The Howler* exist today.

On July 5, 1974, a yellowed frontispiece page from *The Howler*, along with parts from seventeen different bodies, was found in the apartment of sex slayer/occultist Charles Sugar. When asked where he obtained the frontispiece, Sugar said, "Look in a mirror after midnight and ask Vollrath." In prison, Sugar overdosed on his own antiseizure medication. The frontispiece page disappeared.

We hope this Chamomile Kitten™ greeting card has helped "scare" up some fun for you this Halloween!

THANKSGIVING

The woven farm scene on this Chamomile Kitten™ greeting card comes from a traditional Wampanoag Indian blanket motif, which depicts Indians growing corn, squash, and beans under a warm sun. It is a scene of peacefulness and contentment, showing the whole village working together for the betterment of everyone. During the "first Thanksgiving" at Plymouth, Wampanoag Indians—including a Patuxet Indian named Squanto—helped teach the Pilgrims how to farm, fish, and hunt and shared the bounty of that first feast. A TRADITION THAT CONTINUES TODAY AND JESUS AND 9/11.

We hope this Chamomile Kitten™ greeting card helped you "gobble" up some Thanksgiving cheer!

CHRISTMAS

The three wise men bearing gifts on this Chamomile Kitten™ greeting card tells the beloved story of the birth of Jesus—a savior who would bring peace to the world, lift up the poor and outcast, and foster goodwill toward all men, great and small. His gospel of peace is preached today by the heads of wealthy, powerful churches and government leaders.

The gifts of gold, myrrh, and frankincense helped Joseph and Mary flee with the baby Jesus, since King Herod wanted to cut his head off, because of the whole "bringing peace to the world" thing.

We hope this Chamomile Kitten™ greeting card ensures "yule" have a merry Christmas!

CONDOLENCES

The "three lilies on the gravestone" etching on this Chamomile Kitten™ greeting card was taken from a sixteenth-century booklet, *A Gentleman's Amiable Conversement on the Diggeing Up of Freshe Boddies for Experiments Scientifical and Eldritch.*

Throughout England, during the reign of Elizabeth I, dramatic strides were made in the science of diagnostic medicine and the study of the advancement of diseases.

One of the surest ways for a young medical student to view the intricacies and wonders of the human body was to dissect freshly exhumed corpses. By placing three lilies on the gravestone of a recently deceased loved one, a family could signal a "resurrection man" that they were willing to allow the corpse to be stolen, often for a few shillings, which were usually wedged between the earth and the edge of the gravestone, to be collected later.

Of course, with today's modern science, computer simulation technology, and genetic manipulation, the practice of grave robbing for the advancement of medical science is a thing of the past. Today, three lilies placed on a grave is a signal to no one except a wealthy necrophile, many of whom are willing to exchange a fresh corpse for, say, ten thousand dollars in nonsequential traveler's checks, sealed in an airtight bag and wedged between the earth and gravestone.

Ten thousand. Maybe more for a dead teen athlete.

We hope this Chamomile Kitten™ greeting card helps to chase away those "graveyard blues"!

Once I started doing stand-up comedy, I couldn't get enough.

The idea of writing a book, becoming a journalist and then, hopefully, a novelist, couldn't withstand my sudden ambition to craft a perfect dick joke. Five thousand words a day seemed silly when I could bring a room full of drunks together with fifteen perfectly chosen words.

I loved getting to hang out with comedians. After years of record store and movie theater retail, and then temping in offices, it seemed otherworldly that I was suddenly surrounded by a peer group that was clever, quick, and discerning.

I also loved the hacks. Mainly because they helped throw off the public perceptions of stand-up comedy. The average person's view of stand-up comedy was degraded and dismissive. The stuff that was being broadcast on TV—endless brick-background cable shows and watered-down "urban" neon mini-auditoriums with a Lethal Weapon saxophone sting—was truly awful. People—especially dipshit pseudointellectuals who ate up one-man theater shows that were, essentially, reworked hack stand-

up premises—avoided comedy clubs. Maybe they couldn't stand the fact that comedy clubs simply announced what they were—booze-ups with jokes as lubricant.

It reminded me of how literati avoid genre fiction or film snobs sniff at big-budget Hollywood movies or exploitation trash. It was how a lot of musicians treated rap and hip-hop when they first appeared.

But avoiding the trash makes you miss truly astonishing moments of truth, genius, and invention. If you shut your mind to science fiction, you're never going to read The Martian Chronicles *or* The Left Hand of Darkness. *If you think murder mysteries are airport garbage, then you're denying yourself* The Horizontal Man *or* The Daughter of Time. *If movies begin at Ozu and end at Roemer for you, then the subversive brilliance of* Deathdream *and* Rat Pfink a Boo Boo *will leave you in the dust. Die-hard rock-and-rollers will never discover Biz Markie's* The Biz Never Sleeps. *Indie music hard-liners rarely venture into country music territory. Too bad—Dolly Parton's* Jolene *and Waylon Jennings's* Honky Tonk Heroes *are as essential as* Last Splash *and* Yankee Hotel Foxtrot.

And it's the same with stand-up. Yes, I sifted through a lot of garbage in the late eighties and early nineties. But there were always unexpected moments of transcendence and originality. And knowing they were hidden in strip malls made me feel like I was a member of one of the last mystery cults on Earth. Like when the Fat Doctor said, one night's at Garvin's, "I used to work on the suicide hotline but I got fired. People would call up and I kept seeing their point." Then there was Mark Fineman, who said, half to himself, "I don't need to curse to do comedy. But I need to curse to live." Hell, Lord Carrett's non sequitur "You know they won't let you buy a gun if you're crying?" inspired a Holly Golightly song.

A History of America
from 1988 to 1996

As Recounted by the Three Types of Comedians
I Opened for While Working Clubs on the Road

I started my stand-up career in the summer of 1988 at a Washington, DC, comedy club called Garvin's. It's now a gay nightclub called the Green Lantern.

The older, mainstream comedians I worked with laid it out clear and simple for me—you wrote and honed a clean five minutes, went on *The Tonight Show,* got called over to the couch by Johnny, got a sitcom, became a star. There was *no other way to do it.* That was the endpoint and the reward.

Or you could get a gimmick—magic tricks, juggling, song parodies—and make a fortune at colleges and corporate gigs.

And then there were the misguided, passionate rebels. I don't mean the ones who went on to success and relevance. I mean the forgotten ones, the ones for whom things were *way* too personal and their defiance against the "clean five/Carson/sitcom/success" cattle chute made them sputtering, angry shamans of nonconformity. Of course, their fate was stranger and more comfortable than they could have imagined.

I worked with variations of these three comedians until I started headlining full-time in 1996. Then I was lucky enough to get to pick my openers.

I never got to pick my headliners. We had nothing in common, and I truly miss them.

1988

Me: And thank you, folks, *all* of you, for coming out. Let's welcome to the stage Blazer Hacksworth!

Blazer: Hey, how're you doing? That's great. Sooooo . . . 1988, huh? You see how Sonny Bono got elected mayor of Palm Springs? He got *votes,* babe! He should do okay in government. He already knows enough Gypsies, tramps, and thieves, huh? That song, you remember?

Okay . . .

And what's with this "perestroika" that Gorbachev's going on about? Sounds like something I got from that hooker on New Year's Eve! Hey, Gorby, use a little Windex and wipe that grape juice stain off your head, then we'll talk, hah?

Oh, and you saw how C. Everett "Kook" said nicotine was as addictive as cocaine and heroin? That's right, 'cause whenever I want a cigarette, I have to tie

off a vein! "Hey, man, you want to do some rails?" "Of what, Colombian?" "No, Marlboros!" Yeah, right.
Sooo, Quayle's an idiot . . .

*[Four dick jokes and a Jim-from-Taxi impression later,
Blazer leaves the stage to wild applause.]*

Me: All right, now let's give a big welcome to "Wild" Willy Strumston and his Twisted Tunes!
"Wild" Willy [tuning guitar]: Anybody celebrating anything? A birthday? What's this here in the front row, date? First date? Computer-date fuckup?
Okay, here we go . . .

[to the tune of Janet Jackson's "Nasty Boys"]

Nazi
Nazi boys
Did you see the way Kurt Waldheim moo-ooves?
Oh you Nazi boys!
(It's "Kurt," "Herr Waldheim" if you're Nazi)

[to the tune of Don Ho's "Tiny Bubbles"]

Tiny fractures
In the roof of the plane
Makes the ceiling fly off
Makes me shit my pants again

*[Breaks the tune to ask the audience,
"Aloha Flight 243? You heard about this, right?"]*

Me: Ladies and gentlemen, here he comes, "Topical" Tommy Tantrum!

"Topical" Tommy: Oliver North. John Poindexter. I mean, *seriously*. I'm too pissed off to write any jokes about this. You should be too pissed off to *hear* any.

Did you guys read about how the First Republic Bank of Texas has entered FDIC receivership? First off, this is the largest assisted bank failure in history. I guess when they say "federally insured" they mean . . .

. . . Okay, are you people serious? Are you fucking serious? You didn't read about this? What, was *Marmaduke* particularly deep today? This is a primary, load-bearing beam of the coming kleptocracy being laid in front of our fucking eyes and you want to hear about airline food? Okay, fine, you want to hear about airline food. Fine. Here we go. Happy, family entertainment for everyone . . .

[After several pouty, halfhearted airline food jokes and then a longish piece about the August 8 Myanmar "8888" incident, Tommy stomps off the stage.]

1989

Blazer: Whew, what's that smell? Did they fry Ted Bundy again? Or is that the mozzarella sticks? You're a sick crowd, I love that.

Yikes, you see that Clint Malarchuk get his throat cut? *This* guy knows what I'm talking about, and this woman's all, "Tee-hee—what's a Malarchuk?"

He's this hockey player, got his throat cut open by another player's skate. Yeah, I know. Gross. Quick, get some ice!

How 'bout that crazy Khomeini funeral? The body falling into the crowd like that? I felt like I was watching a dude crowd-surf at a punk rock and roll show, huh?

So, the Fox network is showing cartoons in prime time now. *Simpsons* or something? I guess they ran out of people to arrest on *Cops*.

Have you seen these Post-it notes?

"Wild" Willy [*to the tune of Sam and Dave's "Soul Man"*]:

Drive my dad's car
In the driveway
Time for Wapner
Each and every day

Eight pieces
of fish sticks
Counting all
of those toothpicks

I'm a Rain Man!
I'm a Rain Man!

[*to the tune of Lynn Anderson's "Rose Garden"*]

I beg your pardon
But Pete Rose has got a gamblin' problem . . .

"Topical" Tommy: If you don't want to hear about the Keating Five or the Velvet Revolution, now's a good time to take a bathroom break.

So . . .

1990

Blazer: Man, you hear Jim Henson died? Yeah, Kermit was speechless. But seriously, folks, Jim Henson was a genius and he'll truly be missed. There we go—yes, ma'am. A round of applause for Jim Henson.

So, the first McDonald's restaurant opened in Moscow. You want a McBorscht with that, comrade? Two all-beef patties special sauce lettuce cheese pickles onions on a bottle of vodka, huh, Boris? Hey, these people wait in line three days to get toilet paper. I'd hate to see the lines for French fries!

Oh, and you see how Bush raised taxes? Guess I read his lips wrong! Think he's trying to help Imelda Marcos buy some shoes for her trial? If we need money so bad, why don't we get Mayor Marion Barry to sell some crack?

"Wild" Willy [to the tune of the Fine Young Cannibals' "She Drives Me Crazy"]:

He drives Miss Daisy . . .

"Topical" Tommy: Well, I guess you all missed only the biggest merging of media companies in U.S. history with the merging of Time and Warner Communications. I'm telling you, people, we're going to end up under one media umbrella and pretty soon the news and the government will all be brought to you by fucking Frosted *Flakes.*

[A drunk in the audience yells, "They're grrrrrreat!"]

Just perfect . . .

1991

Blazer: Pee . . . !

"Wild" Willy Strumston: Wee . . . !

"Topical" Tommy Tantrum: Okay, first off, his name is Paul Reubens, *not* "Pee Wee Herman," which is a fucking character he plays. I guess the entire country screeches to a halt when—surprise, surprise—an adult male is caught masturbating in a public theater. I mean . . .

[Jokes about the Soviet storming of Vilnius to stop Lithuanian independence, the Visegrad Agreement, and the Milosevic demonstrations in Belgrade; one thrown bottle later, Tommy stomps offstage.]

1992

Blazer: Yeah, so. How're you folks doing? Let's get a round of applause for those Redskins, huh?

Man, Carson retiring, huh? Gonna leave *The Tonight Show.* What's he got, three weeks left there? What do you think, you still think I have a shot? [*Heavy sigh*] So yeah, so Bush, huh? Puking all over the Japanese prime minister like that? Look, if you don't like their trade proposals, say it, don't spray it. And . . .

[Pause]

Of course, next week that joke's going to be a dinosaur. What else have I got here? Mike Tyson raping that chick, something something . . . I think the punch line was going to be something about being "saved by the bell." Oh hey, here's a bunch of stuff about Amy Fisher and Mary Jo Buttafuoco. "I hope this affair doesn't blow up in my face." Well, that's Joe Buttafuoco saying that, now Mary Jo. Who cares anyway, right?

[Sits on stool]

Man, five years ago, the people who made the news seemed to be world leaders or talented people. You know what they should call the nightly news now? *Tonight's Biggest Asshole.*

[Crowd laughs]

Right? Sometimes, I'm walking down the street, and there's a guy with half of his ass showing, screaming at pedestrians. I want to say to him, "Hey, if you'd drop those pants all the way, set one of your turds on fire, and throw it at a baby, you could bump the president off the news tonight." Ah, it's all bullshit anyway.

"Wild" Willy [*to the tune of the Newbeats' "Bread and Butter"*]:

> He likes thighs and eyeballs
> He likes brains and cheeks
> That's what Hannibal Lecter eats
> Every day of the week . . .

"Topical" Tommy: Well, I don't have a guitar like "Wild" Willy, but if I did? And after hearing that bullshit Rodney King verdict? Man, I'd play "Meet the new boss, same as the old boss." This is just typical racist mistreatment of blacks by—

[A black guy, drunk and only half-listening to the show, looks up at the stage and yells, "Don't even go there, motherfucker!"]

No, listen, I'm saying that those white police assholes . . .

[The black guy yells again, "Nuh-uh!"]

I'm on your side, goddamnit!

[They go back and forth for ten minutes, the crowd siding with the black guy, before "Topical" Tommy, shaking, walks offstage, giving the black guy a wide berth.]

1993

Blazer: . . . and another thing about divorce . . .

"Wild" Willy [to the tune of Billy Joel's "We Didn't Start the Fire"]:
>Bill Clinton president
>Intel's making Pentiums
>Showdown at Waco
>Bills lose the Super Bowl

[Tries to rhyme "Don't ask, don't tell" with "Monica Seles," cracks up, and says, "I'm still working on that one."]

"Topical" Tommy: Hey, I've got my problems with the government—that fucking Waco thing? They burn women and children alive and then say they were doing it to protect children? Yeah, right.

But these religious extremists, bombing the World Trade Center? People, we've got to wake up to what the fuck's out there. Yeah, we've got some things here need fixing but if we let a few nut jobs who worship some bullshit desert god scare us into surrender, we're going to find ourselves under sharia law. You know what that is? Well, I'll tell you . . .

[Audience groans. One guy shouts, "U! S! A!"]

1994

Blazer: So, about a year ago, I was at the lowest part of my life. At least I thought I was. Then I found something worse. Dating a Goth waitress . . .

"Wild" Willy: Yeah, so, uh . . . I know I do a lot of silly-ass songs up here and all, and we have fun, right? We're all partying together.

But I was, uh . . .

That Kurt Cobain, blowing his brains out like that? I mean, the fact that he could articulate so much pain in his music, you'd think that'd help him through it. And then you see something like that, where you realize, "Man, sometimes having a creative gift like that does nothing to alter your reality." I mean, if he could write songs like that, and that didn't help him, what fucking hope do we have? Sorry . . .

[Does a shockingly beautiful cover of "About a Girl"]

"Topical" Tommy: NAFTA? Are you fucking *kidding* me?

1995

GARVIN'S NOW UNDER NEW MANAGEMENT
WILL REOPEN IN SPRING OF 1996

1996

I went back to Washington, DC, to work at a new, national chain club in the summer of 1996.

The first morning I was there I did "Wild" Willy's morning show. We joked on the air about the old club and the weirdos who used to come in for open mikes. Off the air, he told me how he was married now and couldn't believe how much he loved the routine of getting up in the morning, doing his show, and then being home in the early afternoon to bring his daughters home from school. He'd stopped writing song parodies years ago, but he hosted regular all-ages shows in Georgetown. He really loved the local band scene. "Can you imagine how cool it would've been to be up in Seattle in the late eighties, instead of slugging away in those shithole comedy clubs?" I couldn't quite agree with him but agreed that Tad, in their heyday, must've been something to see.

I drove around that afternoon in my rental car, visiting friends and seeing the sights. I flipped around the AM dial and found "Topical" Tommy's right-wing radio show. He'd lost none of his anger but, now that he only had to remember six or seven catchall phrases that were guaranteed to set his listeners frothing, he spewed them with a venom that Ian MacKaye would've envied. Maybe all those years of silence, and stares, and dismissal from the crowd had secretly eaten away at him, and now he loved knowing he'd always get a positive response. At the midpoint of the show, he and a caller agreed, angrily, about how the blacks had blown all their chances for social justice and reform after the Rodney King verdict.

"I used to do comedy, and I remember trying to reach out and say how disgusted I was with that verdict, and this idiot in the audience was too stupid to know I was agreeing with him! Started shouting at me and threatening to kick my ass . . ."

The caller said, "That verdict was totally fair! They didn't beat that guy enough!"

"Thank you, *exactly*," said Tommy. I wanted to call him and bring up the Time-Warner merger, but my cell phone wasn't getting a signal.

That night at the club, the manager came back to see me in the greenroom.

"Hey, Blazer!" I said, jumping up and hugging him.

"You want any kind of special intro music?"

I said, "*You* pick something. Your taste is better than mine. You turned me on to the Kinks back when I was an open-miker."

He showed me pictures of his new wife and kids. The son and daughter were athletic and coltish, respectively. The wife was cute, in a sunny blouse and slacks, a tattoo of an ankh on her wrist. The tail of a larger, more elaborate tattoo barely peeked out from the collar of his shirt. The picture was taken at a soccer game in the suburbs.

The emcee introduced me. The Kinks' "Come Dancing" played as I took the stage. I looked out over the room. In the back, standing trim and happy in his sport-coat-over-

T-shirt ensemble, Blazer smiled, lit by the blue light of the bar. *The Tonight Show* was forever gone, forever receded on his horizon. But he'd expanded his endpoint to take in every second of every day, and he'd honed his life down to pure reward.

The Victory Tour

In October 1993 I was a finalist in the San Francisco International Comedy Competition.

Because of this, I got hired by a club owner named Reed* to headline his comedy club in Vancouver, Canada. Which turned out to be in Surrey, which is a suburb of Vancouver the way boredom is a lesser state of excitement. Sorry, Surrey—but I spent the shittiest eleven days of my comedic career in your town and surrounding environs in the immediate company of Reed, the human equivalent of rancid clam chowder.†

---

*Reed isn't the guy's name. I'm also changing the name of his club, which had one of the worst names of a comedy club I've ever heard and is now closed. Keep this in mind when you read the name I give it in this chapter—the real name was worse than the one I made up. I've changed Reed's name on the vague worry he might read this and sue me—a remote possibility, since shortly after my stint at his horrible club he organized a benefit show for a local motorcycle club; a member's daughter was battling cancer or leukemia or something. He then used the money raised to pay off a massive coke debt and flee to Hawaii. Or someplace. No one's sure. If you're not the type to read footnotes, or you are and you think I've given away some deft comedic twist by revealing that Reed was the human equivalent of a spoiled pork sandwich, I'm going to say pretty much the same thing at the end of the paragraph this footnote interrupted.

†See?

At the time, I couldn't have been more excited. Head-lining. In Vancouver. All of my friends gushed about the city, about the cool people and bars and music clubs and the chess players near Burrard Street. I've since visited Vancouver many times and love it.

I visited Surrey in the early fall of 1994, and I would return only if I was tasked to kill a demon to save the world. Maybe not even then. Sorry, Surrey. Sorry, world. Yay, hypothetical demon.

WEDNESDAY, SEPTEMBER 29, 1994

Reed meets me at the airport. He's picking me up, taking me to the Smile Hole, his club. Where am I staying?

"I figured I could take you to the hotel after the show," he says, sniffing wetly every third word.

I say, "Well, I kinda need a shower."

"See, we haven't sold a lot of tickets. We haven't sold *any* tickets. *You* haven't sold a single ticket." Reed can deftly make a declarative statement and follow it with amended, directed blame. "You've got to go do some radio. There's a bunch of drive-time shows that'll go right up before showtime. How bad d'you need that shower?"

"I'd really like a shower . . . I mean . . . okay."

This is my first-ever headlining gig. And I am still naive and paranoid enough to believe that every club and club owner is connected on an invisible "shit wire," where they share stories of diva-like behavior. I think there's a "don't hire" list, always adding a new name, somewhere out in the ether.

We go to a radio station—actually, the second floor of a chewed-on-and-discarded-by-time-and-care office park, where four stations share the cramped second floor. Each "station" is enclosed in stapled-together soundproof sheeting, like gray, indoor teepees. During songs or commercials the deejays pop out like pasty gnomes and shake a soup bowl of sweat off their faces.

Reed greets the first confused deejay and it's clear, instantly, that there never was a scheduled appearance. He's bum-rushing the four stations, like a street barker, and me an exotic orangutan on a chain, hoping someone will let me near an open mike to screech, fling some poop, and say the name of the club. The first three deejays flat-out refuse—they basically back-announce songs—but the fourth bites. I'm pushed into his rock and roll lean-to, and he introduces me to the good people of Surrey.

"Got a funnyman here, going to be at the . . ."

He looks over at Reed, who never told him the club's name. Reed mouths the words "Smile Hole."

"The Wide Hole. Here he is—"

The deejay looks at me and pops his eyes. *Introduce yourself.*

"Oh, uh, Patton Oswalt."

"Making 'em laugh over at the Wide Hole. But right now, the Divinyls want to *touch themselves* . . ." Christina Amphlett's throaty voice fills the teepee and the deejay thanks me for dropping by.

Reed gets lost on his way back to the club and apologizes for not being able to get me over to the hotel in time for a shower.

"Your bags'll be safe in the car here in the lot," he says as we pull up to the Smile Hole, the only thing open in an otherwise abandoned strip mall. "Or we can go over to my place, drop your stuff off there, get you a shower just fine. You never know what a hotel'll charge you for, huh?"

I say I'm okay, let's just go in the club.

The Smile Hole is a small lounge/waiting area, with a bar and a few tables. Double doors lead into the club itself, half again as big as the waiting area. No one's waiting to go in.

The bartender is super-friendly and could not be more excited about the new "ice beer" they've got. "Coors Ice Beer! It's so tasty!"

At this time in my life I'm not really drinking. A combination of misadventures in college and a love of marijuana has caused me to temporarily abstain.

But I've never heard of ice beer, so I take a single sip from the freshly cracked can the bartender plops in front of me. Not bad, but it's all I drink.

"*Iiiice* beer," says Reed, swooping up beside me, with an inflection that makes it sound like he's saying, "Rape's kinda cool, huh?"

Eight people show up. The emcee is warm, friendly, and about as funny as *Shoah*. I take the stage to the sound of, my hand to God, one person clapping *once and only once*, and then I start into my act.

The audience of eight, clustered at two tables in the front, stares up at me with the faces you'd see on mourners at a solemn wake where one of the eulogizers took the stage and farted Wallace Stevens's "The Sun This March." During the course of my set, each of the eight audience members, one by one, gets up to use the bathroom. When they return, they sit down at the farthest table from the stage. By the end of my set, I'm addressing them across an empty room.

Reed takes me to my hotel—the Best Western King George Inn & Suites. My room is an underlit, cream-walled tomb dominated by a bed with a waffle-iron mattress. I take a spitting, resentful shower. I turn on the TV. There's a Jerry Lewis movie dubbed in French. I fall asleep at dawn.

THURSDAY, SEPTEMBER 30, 1994

I wake up at noon.

I make a pot of coffee with the little coffeemaker that's in the room. Now the room smells like a hot, wet hat. The coffee tastes like pants.

I turn on the TV and get my first look at a bizarre Canadian game show called *Acting Crazy*, which manages to make charades even more boring. The one fascinating thing about the show is that the celebrities and citizens play against a depthless, blank void like the prison in *THX 1138* or the in-between zone in *The Matrix*. The only celebrity I recognize is Jack Carter. Years later I'll work with him on the pilot for *The King of Queens*. He'll be replaced by Jerry Stiller once the show gets picked up.

I turn the channel and there's a news report about an inmate who's escaped from a minimum-security mental institution. The newscasters calmly remind everyone that the inmates are allowed to release themselves on their own recognizance. Why, then, do they keep going back to the notion that the inmate has "escaped"? The news report ping-pongs back and forth like this for two more minutes before I switch off the TV and go for a walk.

The walk from the hotel to the club, I discover, is a pleasant ten minutes. I make a note of this for later in the evening. The less time in confined spaces with sniffling, passive-aggressive Reed, the better. And taking in the cold Canadian air is like breathing pure ruggedness.

Thursday night's show draws four people—a group of three, and a middle-aged woman who's clearly been stood up on a date. I realize I take up 25 percent of the space in the universe that my audience takes. I get zero reaction from the crowd, except for a joke whose punch line involves Anna Nicole Smith.

"Cunt," says the lone woman. She doesn't yell the word, or snort it or mutter it. She says it calmly and flatly, like she's politely reminding me of a word I left out of the joke.

I walk out of the showroom with the audience after I say good night. They head straight for the door. I get my jacket and notebook from behind the bar and do the same.

Reed is waiting at the bar, with an ice beer opened for

me. "Oh, I'm good," I say. Reed stares at me, goggle-eyed, like I'm leaving something obvious unsaid. I absolutely can't read his rhythms and don't have the energy to start trying.

I walk back to the hotel. The main road from the club to the hotel doesn't have a sidewalk, and the shoulder is slim and soft. I take a darker side road that I discovered earlier that day, returning from my walk for a sandwich in the hotel restaurant. There are no lights on the sidewalk but I can see the wobbly pinprick of hotel light in the distance. I walk until it gets bigger, go into my room, watch *Chato's Land* dubbed in French, and fall asleep at dawn.

FRIDAY, OCTOBER 1, 1994

"You have to stay and drink tonight."

I'm sitting at the bar, rearranging the order of my jokes. I'm under the delusion that I'm having bad shows because of some cosmic misalignment of words, phrases, and ideas. I may as well have cast runes into a spirit bowl, hoping that the collective heart of the audience would open to my necromantic call. Maybe that's how jugglers do it. Those guys never have shitty sets.

Reed leans closer in. His breath smells like he's been eating Doritos and olives and drinking very little water.

"You have to stay and drink tonight."

I say, "Here? After the show?"

"You just walked offstage last night, and then walked right out of here without hanging out."

"Well, for one thing, the audience hated me." I close my notebook. "And also, I really don't drink."

"You had ice beer on Wednesday!" Reed says, pointing an accusing finger—Hercule Poirot facing down the guilty passengers of the Calais Coach. "You had ice beer, so that means you *do* drink!"

"No, Reed. I tried ice beer. *Tried* it. I *really* don't drink."

Reed's mouth hangs open. "That doesn't make sense."

"It does. I'd never had ice beer before. I wanted to at least know what it tastes like."

And then—and I remember this so clearly—I stop myself from saying this exact phrase:

I want to experience as many different tastes, sights, emotions, conflicts, and cultures as possible, so that I can expand the canvas of my memory and enrich my comedy.

I almost said this to a cokehead in a *Poverty Sucks* T-shirt and acid-washed jeans in a comedy club called the Smile Hole. As if he would answer in kind. As if he wouldn't immediately file that away and share it with his surly, equally coked-out staff. As if I wouldn't spend the next two days hearing variations of "How's your canvas expanding there, Leonardo Van Gogh?" This is the kind of pretentious, oh-so-punchable smacked-ass I still am, with five years of stand-up under my belt.

But I bite down on this and say, "So, uh, yeah. I, uh, wanted to know what it tastes like, but I really don't drink. So . . . so . . ."

Reed said, "Friday night is Party Night number one."*

---

*He actually said this.

"Okay . . ."

"So I need you, after the show, to stay in here and have a drink. We can make you a soda water or a ginger ale or something, and make it *look* like a drink. People see you drinking, then they're going to want to stay and keep the party going. We're not selling . . . *you're* not selling enough drinks," says Reed, reciting the preamble to his mission statement.*

The eleven audience members from the first show are trudging out of the showroom. I'm stationed at a central table, facing the door, a highball glass of soda water with a strategically placed lime wedge in front of me.

At least this audience stayed for the entirety of my forty-five minutes of jokes. They had the fortitude of a homicide detective combing endless perp photos in search of a lurid neck tattoo.

They each pause midstep as they notice me at the table on their way out. Each of them looks at me, glances at the bar, and then doubles their pace out of the club. *We would rather drink quietly somewhere, anywhere, else than imbibe a drop of alcohol anywhere near you and your horrible jokes.*

The last audience member strides out into the bleak Surrey night. Reed slides into a chair next to me and says, "We're thinking of hiring a different headliner for tomor-

---

*Drunks were kings in comedy clubs during the boom years. During the postboom years—1993 being the absolute nadir, if I remember—drunks were gods. Or—who were the fathers of the gods? Titans. They were fucking titans.

row night. Saturday night is Party Night number two. We've got to have good shows here."

I suck on the lime wedge and try to imagine what, in Reed's logic, would constitute a "party night" headliner. He's already imagined that a room full of people burning with hatred (or cold with indifference) for me as a comedian would, upon exiting the show, suddenly think, "Hey, that unfunny asshole is having a drink in the bar! We should have drinks with and/or close to that unfunny asshole!"

I walk back to my hotel on the dim side road, muttering, "Somebody fucking *kill* me," in time with my steps.

SATURDAY, OCTOBER 2, 1994

More news updates when I rise for lunch. The "escaped" mental patient is "not a danger to himself and, more importantly, the public." But his family is making an appeal for him to at least contact them, as he's prone to confusion and could himself be in danger.

I meet my replacement that evening when I arrive for the first show. "Oh hey, c'mere!" says Reed, hopping off his bar stool. He had been sitting next to a huge guy who looks like a beverage distribution agent.

I shake hands with the guy. "This is Gary. We've been . . . how long we know each other, Bo?"

Gary says, "Since this dude couldn't get laid in high school."

"Suck a bone!" says Reed, and they both crack up. Is this guy even a comedian?

"So, where do you get your jokes? Reed says he sees you writing them down in a notebook."

I don't know how to answer this. Gary, like a dispiritingly large chunk of the population, seems to think comedians get their jokes out of books. Does he think I transcribe them to help my memory?

"I write 'em down, too." Gary takes a spiral notebook out of his backpack. Then he produces four or five paperback joke books and a few issues of *Playboy*. He opens the *Playboy* to where he's got a few *Playboy* party jokes marked with yellow highlighter.

"Oh, uh, I write my own stuff."

Gary says, "From where?"

I don't answer. I get a ginger ale and watch Gary transcribe jokes out of the paperbacks onto a separate sheet of paper. At one point, he asks me if a dirty knock-knock joke should come before or after a dirty riddle.

"I'm going to make the riddle sound more conversational, like I'm just saying it," says Gary sagely. "Usually, in a riddle, you ask the question, and then you answer it and the answer's the joke. But see? Here's how I'm going to say it . . ."

I look down at the paper he's slid across the bar to me. He's written:

Did you here [sic] *about the midget porno movie? It's called* Itty Bitty Gang Bang!

Gary says, "That way, it feels more like I'm talking to them. Like Richard Pryor."

Gary kills. *Kills.* A star is born in front of twenty-one people in Surrey that night.

He could not have more of an advantage. For one, the audience is so relieved when I finally finish my half hour, they greet Gary like a redemptive angel come to wash away the acidic taint of my comedy with jokes they already know the punch lines to. Sometimes they recite them along with Gary, and then cheer.

"So, this hooker said, 'I'll do anything you want for fifty bucks' And I said—"

And then the audience swoops in with Gary: *"Paint my house!"*

Ten minutes into Gary's act I head for the door. I want to step outside and get some clean air. The cigarette ban hasn't made its way up to Canada (did it ever?) and the stress of watching me eat it makes the Smile Hole audiences light up with a vengeance. Scalp-to-ceiling-level in the showroom is a solid soup of gray death.

"Where're you going?" Reed lurches between me and the door.

"I'm getting a little fresh air. I'll be right back."

Reed shakes his head sadly. "You should go back in and watch Gary. I think it'd really help you."

"I'll be right back," I say, and shove my way outside.

This is a disturbing, recurring motif in my career. The club owner insisting I stay and watch someone. And Reed resurrecting it brings up a blazing column of anger and disgust.

The club owners never want me to stay and watch anyone *good*. And back when I was an emcee, and had even less courage, they insisted and threatened and seemed to take a weird pleasure in saying, "You're going to sit in this room and find out what *real* comedy is about."

There were the club owners in Williamsburg, Virginia, who made me watch this god-awful hack headliner who sounded like a low-rent televangelist and hadn't changed a word of his act in two decades. Then there was the oily, sneering Philadelphia club owner who, knowing I had a long drive back to Virginia after a late Saturday show, wouldn't pay me unless I watched a black headliner who performed like a retarded Klansman's idea of what a black comedian was. Then, one night in Walnut Creek, California, when the Bay Bridge was closing at eleven P.M., and I politely asked the aggressively forgettable headliner if I could leave after bringing her on, to save me a one-hour drive around the peninsula:

"No, you stay. You've been up there chatting with your other comedian friends in the greenroom, and none of you ever once watched my act. So now you stay."

Well that makes sense, I thought. *You're right to be angry. I've been talking with my lively, creative peers about music we like, and movies, and bouncing jokes off one another, and trying to make our acts better, when I could have been down in the showroom, listening to your grating, monotone pig-voice recite early-eighties bullshit*

about periods, men leaving the toilet seat up, and the dif-
ference between cats and dogs.

Out loud to her, I said, "Okay."

No one ever made me stay and watch Bill Hicks, or
Brian Regan, or Todd Glass or Louis C.K. or Dave Attell
or Warren Thomas or Maria Bamford. Oh wait—*no one*
had to. Comedians naturally went out of their way to
watch and learn from those people.

In the parking lot I witness a fight. Wait, did I say "fight"?
Because it's *not* a fight when there's one dude talking on a
pay phone—a moonfaced, long-limbed-but-still-soft dude
who's not so much talking as nodding and then, a second
later, saying, "Oh, I mean, yes," as the person on the other
end is probably saying, "Did you understand me? Don't
just nod . . ."

And it's really not a fight when the other dude is less a
human and more locomotive incarnate, who barrels forward out of the parking lot and fractures Moon Face's jaw
with a Frye boot. That's how the "fight"—which is a beating—starts and ends. Moon Face drops and pukes blood.
Locomotive stands over him, fists balled, as if Moon Face
is going to spring up and give as good as he got. Moon
Face is instantly drained of any "give" once Locomotive
is done with the "got."

"Scratch my truck bed, motherfucker!" Locomotive
threatens and explains with one sentence.

I'm pretty sure a scuffed truck bed doesn't equal a pow-
dered jawbone, but I don't say anything. I picture Locomotive slicing me in two with his neck muscles alone if

I so much as make a peep. I also picture the audience hearing the carnage from the showroom and, mid-knock-knock joke, piling out into the parking lot. They're met with the sight of me being mulched under Locomotive's boots and another cheer goes up; another star is born. Having witnessed injustice triumph, and someone with the ability to harm choose to do so, I go back inside.

"After this show, I want you guys to shake hands with the audience as they leave," says Reed, stanching a nosebleed with a bar napkin.

Oh Jesus, no, I thought.

Oh Jesus, yes, I have to do it.

If an audience member wants to come up to a comedian after a show, tell him or her they enjoyed it, that they laughed and wish the comedian well, fine. But I am being forced—and it won't be the last time—to position myself at the exit door and shake everyone's hand as they leave. *Whether they want it or not.*

I repelled these audiences sitting in a comfortable lounge with a refreshing drink in front of me, like a living, welcoming liquor ad. Now I have to literally get between them and freedom, and make their last impression of the Smile Hole awkward and hateful.

"I was thinking of doing that anyway!" says Gary.

"That's 'cause Bo wants to keep the party *going*," says Reed, showing me his idea of a withering glance.*

By this time, my opener, now an emcee who only had to

---

*It looked like he'd eaten an unripe banana.

do seven minutes, had adjusted his act. He goes onstage, says, "Who's here to fuckin' party?" The crowd cheers; he shotguns a beer and then belches the word "pussy." Then he brings me up.

I go up in front of a half-full room. The Locomotive sits in the front row. He doesn't look at me as I say hello, since he's too busy plunking a shot glass of bourbon into a mug of beer.

As I plow deeper into my set, and he's got time to sit in the unbroken silence and watch me, I see it—see it on his face—that he realizes I'm the asshole out in the parking lot who saw him sucker-boot Moon Face. My mouth goes dry and I speak faster and faster, not even pausing to acknowledge the silence. I do my half-hour feature set in eighteen minutes and get offstage. The emcee brings up Gary, and I head out to the lounge.

"So, Reed, can I get my check?"

Reed says, "Let's wait till after the show. I need you to stay and shake hands."

"You know, I'll bet they only want to shake hands with G—" I say before he cuts me off.

"After the show," says Reed, pushing past me, behind the bar. He taps his nose at the mulleted bartender and they head out back.

I sit at the bar and scribble in my notebook. I suddenly, very badly, want a drink. Maybe a layer of scotch or two, to act as a numbing shield in case a boot attack should come my way later.

The Locomotive looms into view, past my right shoulder. He's also heading toward the back, where the restrooms are. He doesn't look at me. I bend my head farther down over my notebook.

I jot down two joke premises: "Guy recovering from saying something stupid at a party" and "Horrible things that have popped into my head while masturbating that didn't stop me from masturbating." Underneath them, nothing.

Then a hand as solid as a trailer hitch falls on my shoulder. I look behind me and the Locomotive is staring down from the faraway perch of his own head on his steely neck.

"Your jokes were good. I liked them." He says these words and I realize what he means. *I'm giving you a compliment I don't believe, and you're going to keep your mouth shut.*

"Thank you I'm glad you liked the show thank you," I say. He walks back into the showroom. As he swings the door open I hear Gary's voice say, out of any context, ". . . Chinese! . . ." The door shuts but I hear the crowd roar.

An old man pumps Gary's hand and wheezes with laughter.

"I'm telling you, that joke with the ant floating downstream with a boner, and he's saying for 'em to put up the bridge. That's been a favorite of mine for so long I can't even *tell* you!"

Gary, and me, and the emcee are in an awkward receiving line at the exit door. The crowd files past. There's a bottleneck in front of Gary. A few people are offering the emcee beers. I get terse nods.

At the bar, Reed cuts me a check. "Don't cash this until

Monday. And be back here Wednesday morning. I got a different opener for you on those road gigs." Part of headlining the Smile Hole was staying an extra week and performing at four one-nighters outside of Surrey. Four nights in the chilly countryside, playing bars, restaurants, and God knows what other establishments that Reed has persuaded to plug in a microphone and aim a desk lamp at a stage.

"How's the hotel? It's reasonable?"

"It's nice," I say.

"Got a big sofa down the basement of my place. It doesn't fold out, but it's plenty wide. Bathroom's right upstairs. I'll take you to the supermarket, put any food you want in the fridge."

"I'm good."

Reed says, "Suit yourself." He is inhaling a coke booger as he says it, so I hear "Shoot yourself."

The hotel seems to recede from me every step I take toward it.

SUNDAY, OCTOBER 3, 1994

"Do you mind if I ask you a question?"

I'm sitting in a Subway sandwich shop at one in the afternoon on a Sunday, having a turkey sub and a Diet Coke for breakfast.

While I ordered, one of the waitresses from the Smile Hole came in. She greeted me and actually seemed pleasant, as if we were the survivors of some horrible ordeal in a foreign land and were now back in polite civilization. I could not have looked savory in the harsh sunlight, which made her gesture seem even sweeter.

Now we're sitting at one of the little tables. She's got one of those cold-cut subs that remind me of school lunches. We're eating, and she's telling me about her life in Surrey and how she wants to move to Toronto and maybe be a travel agent.

"I mean, it's cool if I ask you something? Kind of personal?"

"Sure, go ahead," I say.

She asks, "Are you gay?"

"Am I gay? No." *What the hell?*

She washes down a bite of sandwich with her root beer. "Well, why didn't you hit on any of us?"

"What?"

"Me and the other waitresses, we were wondering why you weren't trying to sleep with any of us."

For a second, I'm really flattered. Were they all angling to fuck me, a hellhole comedy club full of young Canadian waitresses? Did I exert some dark gravity up north, the way Superman suddenly had powers when bathed in Earth's yellow sun?

A moment later she shatters my reverie. "I mean, we figured, this guy's the headliner, *one* of us is gonna have to fuck him."

That's right. Not only were these waitresses *not* attracted to me. Not only *didn't* they want to fuck me.

They were resigned to *having* to fuck me.

"Uh, I have a fiancée." The waitress buys the lie. It won't be the last one, I figure.

MONDAY, OCTOBER 4, 1994

This is my first of two days off. No show in the evening. Nowhere to be. I'm waking up in a hotel in a still-strange town, not knowing anyone. Theoretically, I could wake, live my day, and fall back asleep without ever once uttering a word. I feel like an aspirant monk with the diet and sleeping habits of a truck song narrator.

I decide to walk nowhere near the Smile Hole. I want to pretend like I'm truly a silent drifter, and not a comedian who's depending on a paycheck and future one-nighters to pay for the greasy hotel lunches.

So I head east (I think) through the suburbs. It's twelve thirty in the afternoon, and there's a pudgy stranger in an overcoat walking the sidewalks of your neighborhood, Surrey. Head down, brooding, pasty from starches, and blinking in the sunshine. The Dave Clark Five's "Because" begins playing in my head. It's a song I often think of in the middle of the day in an empty suburban street. There's something accidentally sinister under the gliding organ and falling vocal harmonies of that song. Whenever I hear it, I think of the words "daytime menace." For instance, what if someone were peering at me right now, through their curtains, the inside of their house dark and still—maybe they're manic-depressive. And they look outside and see me, the personification of a defeated sigh wrapped in an overcoat, trudging along the uneven sidewalk.

I'd call the police, if it were me.*

It strikes me that, back when I was working the road as an emcee and feature, I would often get put up in a "comedy condo" somewhere in a populated cluster of similar townhomes or apartments, somewhere in the suburbs. A comedy condo was usually a cheap town house that a comedy club would rent and use as a high-end flophouse for whatever comedians were working their club that week. Invariably it would lack a phone, silverware, toilet paper, and comfortable matresses. But it was always flush with the rare scent of haunted hilarity. Thus, during the comedy boom of the eighties, America's suburbs had, on any given weekday (especially Wednesday through

---

*That's what always stayed with me, growing up in the suburbs—any outdoor activity can be viewed from dozens of curtained windows, like royalty peeping out from behind theater box curtains at random amusements. But I also always thought, "You don't know what innocuous action, taken out of context, might affect the life of someone watching you."

As a horrifying example, this story:

A friend of mine had a paper route all through the eighties. It ranged wide and it ranged far—at one point, as far from his house as he could get in our neighborhood.

So one icy morning, he's at the farthest point and is seized by an impending avalanche shit. It's coming, and right soon, and it's five in the morning and there's no toilet in sight.

There's nothing he can do. In the gray morning, he quickly drops his pants and defecates on a stranger's lawn.

Who was in that house? Hopefully happy, sleeping people. But what if, in the depths of winter, there'd been some desperate soul who'd been awake all night, pondering his sorry lot in life, and had decided, around 3:47 A.M., "I'm going to throw open the curtains at dawn and decide whether to go on or end this pathetic charade here and now." Come five A.M., he peers out on God's creation, sees the paperboy shitting on the lawn, and hangs himself with a jump rope in the basement. Worst Beckett play ever.

Friday), lone, bored comedians wandering the sidewalks. Why weren't we foiling break-ins? Or, at least, committing them?

I also realize that, as far as I know, the voluntarily released/escaped mental patient could be wandering around. I haven't seen anything on the news about the poor dude being found. I suddenly want to run into him, go get coffee, find out why he's crazy and why he decided he needed to be free in the gray world of Surrey again. Am I missing some hidden, nurturing vibration, somewhere under Surrey's streets? Can only the insane hear it?

Suddenly the suburbs become sparser, more industrial. Then they're gone. But before I turn back, I realize I'm walking toward a shopping mall.

Shopping malls, in the afternoon on a weekday, are where the braver suburban shut-ins go to pace, and walk, and stare and brood, protected from the sun and rain and always within reach of something sweet or fried. Then there are pretentious assholes like me who go to the mall to watch those people, as if we're going to discover some hilarious new revelation or angle no one's hit upon before. George Romero covered it in *Dawn of the Dead,* but that doesn't stop me from entering, observing, and judging.

Before I go inside I see something heartbreaking, stalled and sky-bound above me: a monorail. A monorail that could take me from Surrey into Vancouver is stalled and out of order, on a track with an entrance that lets out from the second level of the mall.

I tried, earlier that week. A few halfhearted attempts with sympathetic-looking staff members of the Smile

Hole, me saying, *Hey—we ought to all go into Vancouver after the show!* And then, variations on the same response: *Fuck that, Vancouver's full of weirdos. S'just hang at the bar here.*

Another repeated motif in my life—being in a boring city close to a fun one, with no money or transportation, and surrounded by people happy with the boredom. Sterling, Virginia, kept me out of reach of Washington, DC. San Antonio, Texas, was full of comedy club bar staff who hated the "faggots" up in Austin. And now Surrey—who needs Vancouver when there's ice beer and free pretzel 'n' nut mix?

Inside the mall, in the distance, I hear singing. I follow it to the food court.

On a stage surrounded by the various food vendors, random Canadian citizens audition to be in a commercial for something called Turtles, which appears to be some sort of chocolate cookie snack. To the tune of "My Blue Heaven," people have to sing a song about Turtles. The refrain is "I . . . loooooooove . . . Turtles!" I get a large coffee, sit at a table, and watch.

The people auditioning, and the crowd watching, have more joy and playfulness than all five shows I did at the Smile Hole. Whereas I was this driven, nervous, ambitious young comedian with something to prove and burrowed deep inside my own head, the auditioners are unpretentious, self-effacing, and unashamed. Whereas my audiences were drunk, surly, and closed off to any sort of comedy except the shitty kind they saw on TV, the audience in the mall food court shifts gears effortlessly and enjoys everyone who goes up. A little girl does a whispered, spooky version of the song, and the crowd loves it. An old man spreads his arms to emphasize every note, articulates the words through a gap-toothed smile, and ends his song with a little "Yip!" The crowd loves that, too. The performers have no expectations for the audience, and the audience has no expectations for the performers. I spend an hour watching people sing about chocolate cookies, and all of them get closer to the way I should be performing comedy than I have in the last five years.

I walk back to my hotel. I read for a bit, have dinner, and switch on the TV. I am, at this point, completely addicted to a Canadian version of the show *Cops*. This one features no bleeping of curses, lots of drunks, and arrestees who, once they realize they're going to be on TV, ham it up for the camera. Even the cops seem amused by it all. I imagine the escaped mental patient is somewhere right now eluding a squad of gentle, smiling cops and singing to himself about chocolate cookies.

TUESDAY, OCTOBER 5, 1994

Every inch of the floor is covered in clothes.

I've found a secondhand clothing store near the hotel, and I'm looking for a jacket. My overcoat, a green Russian greatcoat-style monstrosity, is starting to feel like constant luggage. I bought it in college. I'm slow to buy new clothing—I tend to buy twelve of the same T-shirts, three pairs of jeans, some button-up shirts to wear over the T-shirt on fat days, and then a light coat and a heavy coat. Simple. Some days I envy Winston Smith in *1984*—same overalls every day? Perfect.

Now I want something in between. I don't know what I'm looking for, but when I walk through the doors of the Second Chance boutique, I'm delighted.

It's essentially a retail space where people bring in clothes to donate or, I guess, sell. Either way, they all end up in the same place—strewn all over the floor. I'm not kidding—there isn't a single clothing rack or shelf in the place. There's a checkout counter, where a lumpy woman reads a paperback copy of *North Dallas Forty*. And then, all the way to the back wall, are clothes. Shirts, pants, jackets, dresses. It's like a gentle hurricane politely let itself in, blew everything off the walls, and left.

There are little towpaths through the floor of cloth-ing. I walk them like a meditation maze. There's some-thing about everything laid out flat at your feet—you can tell, instantly, what will fit and what won't. It was as if I floated outside memories of myself passed-out drunk in college and kept a sense memory of my dimensions.

And there it is: a black leather jacket, like Alan Arkin wore in *Wait Until Dark*. Mid-thigh length, cut like a sport coat, with flapless pockets and three big buttons up the front. It's perfect. I don't even try it on. I take it up to the counter, give the cashier ten dollars Canadian, and slip it on once I'm outside. It doesn't feel like a jacket I bought. It feels like a jacket I left in Surrey, in another life, and have just now recovered.

Back in my room, the jacket keeps paying off dividends. A paperback I have of *Nightmare Alley* fits perfectly in one pocket. In the other, *Carioca Fletch*. The pockets of the overcoat never quite held books correctly, always spitting them out like watermelon seeds if I sat in a cramped airline seat.

I feel like I can survive the next four days.

WEDNESDAY, OCTOBER 6, THROUGH SATURDAY, OCTOBER 9, 1994

The opening act who drives me to the four one-nighters compares everything he sees with pussy. Wednesday's show is at a diner. A drunk comes in midway through my act and demands I start over. Thursday we're at a banquet hall and two separate girls on two separate dates throw up. Friday we're at a bar and when I sit at the bar and try to read *Carioca Fletch* the bartender says, "This is a bar, son," and then tells me to put the book away. Saturday we're at a Chinese restaurant and there's vomiting and a fight.

But I'm safe in my leather jacket, and we both return Sunday morning vomit-free.

SUNDAY, OCTOBER 10, 1994

My hotel room is padlocked. *Padlocked*. The rest of my luggage and my return plane ticket (for a flight I have to make in two hours) are inside. Behind a padlock.

I call Reed and, miraculously, he's at home. I need him to come over to the hotel and get the door unpadlocked so I can go home.

"Well, I'll come over," he says with this doubtful tone that tells me something bad is about to begin.

He shows up and here it is: he wasn't paying for my extra days.

"You know, I made it very clear to you that you could either stay in the hotel on your days off or come stay at my place."

I said, "Yes, you gave me both choices, and I chose the hotel."

"But that means you were agreeing to pay for the hotel room."

"No, it doesn't," I say. "Because that was never stated when you gave me the so-called choice."

"Well, it was *implied*," says Reed, teaching me a new word.

"No, you didn't even come close to implying it," I say. "You talked about getting some food for me to put in your fridge, and that there was a shower and TV. But you never said, 'If you stay at the hotel, you will have to pay for the room.'"

Reed says, "Well, I'm saying it now."

"Well, now's too late. My passport, my ticket, the rest of my luggage is in the room."

"Well, I don't have the money to get it out."

I'm near tears at this moment. But I also get an unexpected burst of courage, and here's what it feels like:

I don't care anymore if this guy hates me or bad-mouths me to other club owners. Because now—and I've never felt this before—I actively *want* him to hate me. It becomes imperative, for my self-worth, that an asshole like Reed actively loathe me. If someone like this were to like me, to like my comedy, and to like the way I conduct myself professionally, it would mean I suck as a person.

I've encountered this a few times since then. Not very often. But there are those rare occasions—and they're bracing, freeing sensations when they occur—when you absolutely crave someone's disapproval and disgust. You can see it actually helping your career, your social relations, and your life if it becomes known that this person thinks you're shit. It's happened so far with a handful of people, but . . . Reed? Take a bow, you coke-soaked ogre. You were the first.

"I don't think you know what 'imply' means," says Reed.

Now my voice is flat, unhurried, and, I can see, frightening to Reed. "You need to pay for the extra days. You need to pay for them now, so that I can get my luggage, ticket, and passport and fly home. And you need to take me to the airport."

Reed stares at me for a moment. "You didn't pull in very big crowds."

"Please get the padlock off my door so I can go home, Reed."

He grudgingly goes to the desk clerk to see if they can temporarily take the padlock off the door. He'll call my manager later, see about getting reimbursed for the money he's got to pay.

Then the desk clerk saves me.

"This room hasn't been paid for *at all*."

Reed's been caught. What the fuck was his plan? To somehow talk me into paying for my entire time at the hotel, after the gig was over? To hold my remaining luggage hostage? What if I'd taken everything out of the room when I'd left for the four nights out on the road? Reed had the tactical foresight of a goldfish.

Before Reed can say anything I look at the desk clerk. "Sir, I am a comedian who just completed his contractually agreed-to performance at both this man's club and four single-night performances. I was told the room would be paid for, and the balance isn't my responsibility. I'm asking you politely to remove the padlock so I can collect my things and then go to the airport. This is not my financial obligation."

I sound like a desperate robot. The clerk removes the padlock; I swoop up my bag, ticket, and passport and then hop into Reed's car. I watch him, through the hotel lobby's windows, halfheartedly talk with the clerk.

Three separate times Reed points out the window at me. His face is a pinched mask of rage.

We drive to the airport in silence. I hop out, and he starts to say, "So, your manager—"

I slam the door and walk through the airport's automatic doors. Behind me, in a cloud of coke-infused snot, Reed drives away.

Sitting at the gate, suddenly sweating and shaking from the confrontation, I look up at a TV showing the news. The lead story is about the "escaped" mental patient—

who turns out to be a multiple ax murderer. He comes from extremely wealthy parents who, trying to lessen the taint on the family name, had their son committed to the voluntary facility, purely for the bragging rights of saying their son wasn't really a criminal.

And he's been apprehended—early that morning—behind the Best Western King George Inn & Suites.

I'd walked four nights, back and forth down an unlit path, muttering, "Somebody fucking *kill* me," in a rhythmic, persuasive cadence. With an ax murderer on the loose.

True story, folks.

FULL DISCLOSURE

Stuff I did on the Internet while writing this chapter:

➤ Played some space shooter game with the sound off while listening to podcasts

➤ Printed a recipe for Welsh rarebit, then decided not to make it

Those Old Hobo Songs, They Still Speak to Us

Got a pecker made-a cigarettes
And eight dead wives
My ass is full of soup
—Opening lyrics of "Squirrel House Christmas,"
Clemm Dogderbek, c. 1926

The song-story tradition of North America's "hobos" (a slang term that combines the words "hope" and "bowl of beans given to me for free by a woman who then initiated intercourse") is rich and worthy of deep study. The above lyrics, recorded by traveling archivists, are a sterling example.

Clemm sings of a "Squirrel House Christmas," which is a hobo-only holiday during which a group of hobos— or a single tramp—would ingest his body weight in alcohol and attempt to climb a tree ("squirrel house") and throw pinecones at pedestrians ("Christmasing"). The vivid description of Clemm's reproductive organ as being

composed of cigarettes has a playful origin, since many hobos would trade a glimpse of another hobo's penis for a single cigarette. Since Clemm uses the plural term for "cigarette," he is boasting that he either

a) has a large penis (and can thus demand a higher penis-view-to-cigarette ratio) or
b) receives many requests from other hobos to view it.

If *b* is the actual truth, then Clemm is further insinuating that his penis is free of the usual "summer plums" (chancres), "tuft tigers" (pubic lice), or "yipe stripes" (bruises brought about by beatings from railyard bulls or, more often than not, punching one's own penis from sheer boredom).

"Eight dead wives" is not as morbid or violent a term as it first appears.

A "live wife" is a slang term for any debt owed to a fellow hobo. Since many hobos were forced to repay debts with sexual favors ("wifing"), Clemm is saying that he's paid off eight recent debts ("eight dead wives") and is feeling victorious ("my ass is full of soup").

Compare the rollicking lyrics of "Squirrel House Christmas" with the more elliptical, tone-poem quality of "Toenail" Timmy Trimblish's "Springtime":

Bug-dick, bug-dick
Oatmeal pants
Salami whore's twat box
Fill it up with ants

Dead mouse pecker puppet
Wave it at a church
Eat a peck of pickle berries
Then shit

Whereas Clemm's song is comical and boasting in nature, Toenail evokes a thoughtful, reflective quality.

Spring is a time of renewal in nature, and that goes doubly for hobos. One of the first signs of spring is bees, traveling from flower to flower as they gather nectar and unwittingly pollinate a summer's worth of blooms. It is a sight that inspires poetic reveries—dreamy, hopeful inner vistas that remind us we are all, great and small, connected to the diurnal cycle.

"Bug-dicking" is a hobo term for this process. Note this excerpt from the rarely performed play *Shoebox Serenade*:

LITTLE GIRL: Look at the bumblebee on the pretty flower!

["Mudtoe" Simmons emerges from a row of bramble bushes, with several bleeding cuts on his exposed belly.]

MUDTOE: That bug's dicking the flower in the petal-pussy! Bug-dicking!
MOTHER: Get away from my child!

"Oatmeal pants" is a clever bit of "hobo code" and actually means "short-sleeved shirt." Hobos were forever afraid of people asking precisely what they had in their pants, so they'd refer to any trousers they might be wearing as a "coconut shirt" ("coconut" = "white") and any

shirt as "pants." "Oatmeal" is hobo rhyming slang for the color blue.* Thus the lyric "oatmeal pants" is a way of saying, "I'm wearing a blue shirt, and there's no reason for you to take any interest in what may or may not be in my trousers."

"Salami whore's twat box" needs no explanation.

"Fill it up with ants" is a term meaning "get some soup started" or, more generally, "begin preparations for dinner." Trimblish has secured the company of a young lady and is about to make some dinner—possibly barley or millet in warm water, a celebratory dish for hobos. One can imagine Trimblish's quiet joy as he fills an empty fireman's helmet with sun-warmed water from a poorly guarded

---

*Most hobos were, for some reason, insistent that "oatmeal" rhymed with "blue."

dog dish, slowly digging the millet or barley grains from his pocket (his "coconut shirt" subterfuge has paid off!) while, nearby, his companion gnaws lustily on her salami with her remaining strong molars. Hobos could be crass, but they never lacked sentiment.

"Dead mouse pecker puppet" also needs little explanation, except in the way of social function. Once the deboned and scraped-clean mouse carcass was fitted over a hobo's reproductive member, he would entertain other hobos with "puppet theater"—usually retelling various hobo folktales. The "mouse puppet" would play various roles, such as:

"Half-Gone" Johnny Strong in "Snoozin' on the Tracks"
"Fist-Width" Petey Fishbein in "Jailhouse Prom"
"The Bludge" in "Stool Pit"

Performing the same known-by-all folktales for other hobos (who would often interject random, personal embellishments or, more often than not, try to box the mouse puppet) could become tiresome. Where to find a new, unversed audience who could delight in these whimsical tales with the innocence of a child? Where could a large group of people be found gathered together? The answer can be found in the lyric "Wave it at a church."

"Pickle berries" are pencil erasers.

FULL DISCLOSURE

Stuff I did on the Internet while writing this chapter:

➤ Typed "Ilkey Moor" into Google and found a picture of
what might be a goblin
➤ Read the trivia section on the imdb.com page for *The
Breakfast Club*

I Went to an MTV
Gifting Suite and All I Got
Was This Lousy Awareness
of My Own Shallowness

I got invited to the MTV Style Lounge a few years ago. It's the first and last "gifting suite" I'll ever go to.

You know what a "gifting suite" is, right? Remember that episode of *The Sopranos,* the one where Chris-tu-pha goes with Ben Kingsley to a gifting suite out in Hollywood and can't believe all the free goodies they're piling onto these celebrities? Then later he punches Lauren Bacall?* Yeah, that one. It's a room or, in my case, an entire fucking house full of free shit they give away to celebrities.

I'd read about gifting suites before. *US Weekly* seems to have a permanent branch of their reporting staff covering them. Hey, celebrities worked hard to become insanely wealthy and famous, right? Don't they deserve some ret-

---

*Chris-tu-pha, not Ben Kingsley.

177

roactive free shit, to make up for all the years they had to survive on a standard living wage?

Also, the term "gifting suite" has this sinister, Orwellian quality. Like something Warren Ellis or Grant Morrison would come up with as a creepy throwaway bit of dialogue in one of their mind-bending stories. Maybe a "gifting suite" is a torture room or a lab where they infect subjects with biological agents, shit like that.

It still wouldn't be half as horrifying as the actual suite I visited.

First off, there weren't a lot of actual "celebrities" there. The fact that I was invited should let you know the cultural cachet of the attendees. Well, maybe there were some big, actual, photo-worthy celebrities attending later, but not when I got there. I got there at noon on a Friday.

That's when the "celebrities" consisted of asterisks like me and people who had *fast-forwarded*.

"Fast-forwards" describes a specific substratum of the Los Angeles population. These are people who, even though they don't have a shred of talent or even a joyful curiosity about film, music, or theater, have a ravenous appetite for the rewards those three pursuits bring. So they've decided, *Fuck it, I'm going to fast-forward to the rewards stage.* Part of the "rewards," in their estimation—and this is beyond the goodie bags, chef's tables in restaurants, and access to exclusive nightspots—is getting to treat everyone like shit.

Assholes. Assholes in bespoke clothing, distressed jeans, and artfully faded concert T-shirts barking and sighing at everyone and everything around them. *Bitches.* Bitches who stomp down Melrose in week-old fashions, already furious that there's new stuff on the racks, and I swear to God I'd better get personal service when I walk into that goddamn boutique or this boba tea's going in someone's face. *Shitheads*. Shitheads who were confident that every repeated catchphrase that left their freshly balmed lips was brilliant or perfect for the occasion. Their hands were always, subtly, at half-mast, ready to post up for a high five when they successfully repeated the watered-down hip-hop slang they'd acquired.

You pulled up to a valet station on Benedict Canyon, where a driver took your car away, and you boarded a huge SUV, which then took you a little farther up a hill to where the "gifting suite residence" was. Well, this was paradise for the Assholes, the Impatient Bitches, and the Fearless Shitheads. They got to complain about having to leave their expensive cars, they got to bitch to the reception girls about having to stand in the sun, they got to roll their eyes at the SUV, which, apparently, was "ghetto" and "last year." Wow!

Maybe these men and women realize how short a window they have where, coiffed and dressed, they've still got tight, young-enough faces to fool people for the three seconds it takes for them to squeeze beyond the velvet rope. Hot, tan, blond girls who are structurally and philosophically hideous. Buff, gelled, open-collared boys who can't read and constantly text.

This is not a screed against Los Angeles. Los Angeles is five of the best cities in the country, and three or four of the worst.

My friend the brilliant comedian Blaine Capatch said Los Angeles is eight or nine different cities. You have to pick the right ones to live in. I was spending the afternoon in the part of Los Angeles that is Sunset Boulevard west of Crescent Heights. It's Robertson Boulevard between Beverly and Olympic. Both of these areas could be napalmed, and the IQ and talent level of the city would triple.

I hadn't even reached the house yet, and my self-loathing was bubbling and curdling in my stomach. The fact that I'd accepted the invitation revealed a nascent shithead streak that ran to my core. I know it's still there. I've got to live with it.

My agent had said, "You wanna go to the gifting suite? MTV invited you." I responded with my lizard brain. *Free stuff! Blaaaaaaarghhhh! Give me free stuff!* Like a galumphing goat of greed and gimme, I accepted.

Now I felt like shit. But it was too late. The SUV pulled up to the gifting suite residence, and a clutch of asswipes pushed their way past me from the backseat, scanning the landscape like velociraptors for someone who wasn't moving fast enough for their taste.

I got my ID from the receptionist and found out that the gifting suite was put on by some organization trying to raise awareness for AIDS. I clung to this fact like a life raft in a sea of wrong.

I was immediately led into a high-ceilinged chamber where an Adidas rep was giving away custom shoes. A flat-screen TV was set up, connected to a web page where you can design your own sneakers. He shoved a pair of size 11 basketball hi-tops into a canvas bag and told me,

"Check out the website at home when you get a chance. It rocks."

The second those shoes went into the bag my brain started screaming, "*Out!* I want *Out!*"

It comes down to this: *I love money.* I love success and fame even more. But I worked very hard to get money so I can *pay for things myself.* That's what turns me on and makes me happy. Having shit handed to me by surly hipsters, or people whose mouths smile but eyes don't, is bad for the soul.

But no, I still had to do penance. Led around by a tightly smiling escort, I had to visit ghastly jewelry dealers; shitty tequila salesmen; loads and loads of iPod accessories, stationery, and facial cream concerns; and two sad-looking hotties from a restaurant called Pink Taco. "Pink Taco"— get it? It's a rude slang term for "pussy"! But it's Mexican food!

"We're opening a new place in Century City. It's going to be off the hook. It'll be super-crowded and, like, the place to be," intoned one of the girls, adjusting her baby-doll halter.

Super-crowded. That's the habitat. That's where these people thrive. I was surrounded by women waiting for someone to cut in front of them. Their upper lips were permanently curled, and their jaws were always half-relaxed, ready to fully snap open and let fly with a hellish trumpeting of unrighteous fury. Their lives are spent crowded in front of the Griddle on Sunset for breakfast, fighting for a treadmill at Crunch, jostling for lunch at Chin Chin, and spending long, pointless nights outside of Hyde or the

Spider Club. I'd just discovered a remote bar on Magnolia in Burbank. Cool, dark interior, plush booths, and never crowded. A terrific jukebox. Scotch and pretzels. One of my favorite places to eat is BLD, which can get crowded, but there are plenty of windows of opportunity to eat and read and not be slapped against the rest of humanity like pigs. And I walk, for hours, in the space and cool of a nearby park.

Hell on earth for the Assholes. If there isn't the potential for a screaming match over a shoulder nudge, *it isn't life.*

While I was waiting for the SUV to take me back to my car, I got waylaid by an assistant from MTV's *Pimp My Ride.* You know what a pimp is, right? He's a dude who tricks, frightens, or flat-out bullies a woman to fuck other men for money, which she then gives to him. Oh, and it's also an adorable slang phrase. There's a doggy grooming spa near where I live called Pimp My Pooch. Someday there will be a baby boutique called Rape My Bassinet.

Anyway, the assistant was showing me some of the cool cars from the show, which they had in the house's massive garage. And by the way, this was not a house where people lived, raised families, hosted friends, built memories. This was a sprawling, unwelcoming residence that was rented out for brainless rap videos or shitty TV shows where they needed a remorseful but sexy drug dealer's pad. You get to see a lot of gifting suite denizens as background extras in these.

So he was showing me a "party van" they'd outfitted with an extendable "Wheels of Steel" and minibar. It was kind of nice. Wow, someone had actually, you know, *created* something. Had used skill and talent to craft something kind of new. My heart warmed for a moment.

"Yeah, we had this thing at a Ja Rule record release party, and we hired a fuckin' midget to serve drinks out of the side. And this one bitch . . ."

But I couldn't hear him anymore. My heart had snapped shut. Even the few good things in this world were splashed with wet ugliness.

I rode the SUV back down and waited for my car. At one point, a blond-haired nobody with perky tits and bad skin got in my face and said, "Is there a long wait at the house? Or do I get to go right in?"

"You're not missing anything," I said, and she managed to sigh and sneer at the same time. The sneer made her zits flare under her spray-on tan.

I drove to the House of Secrets, got comics, and then ate a quiet, yummy turkey sandwich at the half-empty Tallyrand on Olive Avenue, and thought about how much I suddenly missed my grandma Runfola.

Anybody want a pair of size 11 Adidas?

Mary C. Runfola
Explains Her Gifts

EIGHTH BIRTHDAY

A picture of Chuck Yeager
signed to someone named "Jimmy"

Grandma Runfola: Well I know how much you liked that *Space Battles* movie. And I thought . . . yes, all right, dear, yes, *Star Wars.* So anyway, I was at this rummage sale and they had a table—well, one man there had a table, and I don't think he was with the rummage sale people because he had his table set up a little bit off to the side. Well, he had two tables. One table was all these photographs of celebrities. And the other table had a large beach towel over it. And I couldn't see what was under the beach towel but I was standing there looking at the different pictures and every now and then a young man would come up to the man selling pictures. And all of these young men either had these really close crew cuts or blond hair and they looked like if a punch in the face could get up

185

and walk around and wear clothing. And the man selling pictures would let them lift the towel and it looked
like all these knives and Nazi stuff. And the punch-in-the-
face men would buy a knife or a patch. Maybe they were
actors buying props for a stage show.

Oh, but anyway, Chuck Yeager. Well, you liked *Sp*—
yes, dear. *Star Wars*. Well, you liked that movie so much
and did you know Chuck Yeager was kind of a space
pilot, like that Han Solo fellow? Oh yes, I know Han Solo,
your grandmother didn't just fall off the pickle truck. Han
Solo and Mr. Spock and Robbie the Robot and everyone.
Well, the signature meant that Chuck Yeager actually held
this photo, which makes it even more valuable.

ELEVENTH BIRTHDAY

The cassette case for AC/DC's *For Those About to Rock*
with a *Best of Steppenwolf* cassette inside of it

Grandma Runfola: Well, you wouldn't believe it. There
was a blind box sale, where you buy a box for fifty cents
and you get whatever's in it. Except this box had been
under a leaky drainpipe, so one of the corners was soaked
and kind of caving in. So I talked the man down to a *dime,*
can you imagine? Inside there were twelve baby bibs that
I gave to your cousin Jesse—maybe he could wipe something down with them in the summer? And then there was
this cassette and it looks like a rock band. Well, when I

opened it up it was only half a cassette and these three big, dead beetles, which I guess eat plastic, or maybe not because it's almost like they ate the plastic and then died. But then this other cassette was in the box, inside a bag of marbles, so I put it inside this case. It's got "wolf" in the name of the band and on the case there's a cannon, and what's more rock and roll than a wolf and a cannon about to shoot?

EIGHTEENTH BIRTHDAY

An old shovel (no, really—an unbelievably old shovel)

Grandma Runfola: Oh, it's an antique, you can't use it. That handle's just a giant toothpick at this point.

TWENTY-FIRST BIRTHDAY

Volumes 2, 3, and 7 of a twelve-volume *Works of Thackeray*

Grandma Runfola: I thought I remembered seeing on TV once that he only wrote three books. Oh well. Won't it be fun hunting down the other books? It'll be a mystery to solve, like that *Hunt for Red October* movie!

TWENTY-FIFTH BIRTHDAY

A lantern shaped like an owl

Grandma Runfola: Do you remember the Frasers? They had the daughter who did gymnastics and the son who went to college and kept hugging other boys and now he's a swimming coach? Well, they knew these people who were having an estate sale last summer so we all went out there—me and the two Fraser parents, not their kids. So we get there and it turns out the estate sale was the day before, and we'd driven all this way. We couldn't believe it. So on the way back, driving back home, we see this antique shop, and it's the most hodgepodge-looking place I think I ever saw. And we had to go in. And I got this lovely hourglass that on the one side it looks like an egg but the other side the glass is square, like a box. And Jeannie—that's Mrs. Fraser—she bought a flag for a country; I think it was Iceland. And Mr. Fraser didn't buy anything but he loved all of these old toy soldiers they had, only he said, "I don't have the space to keep them anywhere." But he sure loved them. And when we left it was raining and we weren't too sure about going down the road we were on because it was getting muddy, so we stopped at a Hardee's and when we were sitting down with our sandwiches I realized I'd left the hourglass back at the store. So we asked the Hardee's if we could use their phone, since it was a local call, and they were so nice and we called and the man from the shop drove all the way down to the Hardee's and gave me the hourglass. He was the nicest man and you could tell the people at the Hardee's knew him and he must be popular, which is no surprise seeing how he treats his customers.

The owl I bought at a Rite Aid.

THIRTIETH BIRTHDAY

Grandma Runfola: Your mother said to get you a Banana Republic gift certificate.

Appendix A:
Erik Blevins

I used to have an office at a film production company. I wasn't working on anything in particular there—just a pilot for Comedy Central that went nowhere. But during that time the production company had an empty office, where my writing partner and I would go in, and bang the pilot script around, and try to stay off the then-infant Internet. Downloading porn was even more time-consuming over a chattering, spitting modem line.

I liked going into an office. Especially the acoustic-tile ceiling, fluorescent-light expanse the production company occupied. It was gray and white and anonymous. It had the feel of an insurance company, and I could imagine the script I wrote on my clattery old desktop Mac was a subversive tome I was sneaking in between denying workman's comp claims. The coffee tasted like a quota and the doughnuts thunked into my stomach like time cards.

But my favorite part about that office were the freelance submissions from would-be screenwriters. I wanted to write films myself. I was, in fact, also working on an original screenplay I owed to Paramount as part of a blind script deal.

It wasn't very good. By that, I mean, it was inept and juvenile.

It sucked.

But these freelancers . . . wow! Their work made my C-minus efforts feel like the scripts Preston Sturges dreamed of writing, had he more talent.

And they never submitted *actual, completed screenplays*. They sent in their idea of a film treatment—as if the idea itself would leap off the page and spike a hunger in whomever read it to see this vision realized, no matter the cost.

I began collecting these treatments the way certain of my friends collected Chick tracts or bad art. It didn't take me long to feel a genuine fondness and affection for these hobbled, brain-damaged orphans, these children of men and women who dreamed so much bigger than their talents gave them the right to. There were many days, working on the pilot or the Paramount script, when I realized I was simply trying to finish a particular scene, to just fucking get it done without any real passion or invention of risk. Can't Point B get here quick enough so I can go on to the next thing?

And I'd have to remind myself that, for all the giggling I did over the typo-heavy, grammatically swoopy freelance submissions I was piling into my drawer to snicker at— those film treatments never tried to simply "get by." Every single scene, every moment and movement they imagined, would someday, surely, be projected on a theater screen somewhere—they went for broke, without fail. Of course, they went for broke the way someone taking a 20 mph corner at 80 mpm goes for broke before ending up a blazing wreck in a ditch. But wasn't that better than what I was doing, in my laziest, most frustrated moments?

It wasn't long before I started writing my own "treatments." I did it to amuse my partner and other people in the office. They were fun. They took, at most, five minutes to write. They were long blog posts I printed up and passed around. My comment threads were my actual coworkers, ho-hoing and wanting more.

Before I knew it, I needed these things as warm-ups. Before any writing session, I'd bang out a treatment. Horror, romance, action, or supernatural—I wanted to see if I could cover as many genres as I could.

One of the other things that fascinated me about all of these horrible treatments was how deeply personal they were. Despite the ineptness of the writing—or maybe because of it—their writers' values, and peeves, and hopes shone through far stronger than any seemingly "personal" piece of screenwriting. Charlie Kaufman, Richard Price, or Miranda July have never been as exposed, raw, and blunt as the anonymous writer who submitted a treatment about all of the world's teenagers being forced to live on the moon and fight arena battles for the amusement of the "older, more responsible generation." I hope he and his son worked out their differences without any bloodshed. Or the building of a rocket.

There are certain movies—the films of Ed Wood Jr., Russ Meyer, Frank Ripploh, Albert Brooks, Lina Wertmüller, and Andy Milligan, especially—that are as much a repeated autobiography of the filmmaker as they are about anything having to do with the characters or story on-screen.

So, as my own self-created "treatments" piled up, I began to see a portrait emerge of the writer. Someone impatient with set-up and craving variety (why have one monster in a film when you can have eight?) and escalating violence. Oh, and boobs.

In other words, me, at my id level. I gave my movie-lover id a name—Erik Blevins—and started running his treatments on the then-infant bobanddavid.com website. People seemed to like them. They floated around the Internet for a while, and then vanished. I left the office, the Erik Blevins drawer became a folder on my computer, and that was that.

Many years later, I wrote this book.

I didn't realize, when I started, how fascinated I still was with different forms of writing—whether they're scholarly papers (the chapter on hobo songs), film production notes ("Punch-Up Notes"), or wine lists. They all have different tones and personalities.

Being an insecure, first-time author, I wasn't confident enough to just flat-out write a collection of personal essays. The chapters like "Peter Runfola" and "The Victory Tour" were terrifying for me to write. I've gotten comfortable enough onstage as a comedian to speak with my own voice, without having to ape anyone else or hide behind a character. But it took me two decades to get to that level of comfort. Now I was entering a completely new arena, and one where I didn't have the luxury of going up night after night, honing and refining what I do. Words on paper, no matter how many times they've been rewritten and edited, are forever.

If I get to write another book, I think I'll be comfortable enough to simply write like myself, for better or worse. Writing years are more compressed than comedian years, at least in terms of development.

But I feel like I owe Erik Blevins. A short tribute, if you would.

So what follows is a handful of the "best" of Blevins. There's really not much that needs to be said by way of explaining what these are. Movie studios have endless files of treatments and pitches just like these, mailed in randomly, half-coherent hopes that the visions their writers saw in their heads somehow made it to the page. Part of me thinks, were I an insane billionaire, I'd shoot some of these films, text unchanged. But I hope I'd stop myself and build a school instead.

Ladies and gentlemen, Erik Blevins:

SLADE RIPFIRE:

Punch to Kill

Treatment

By Erik Blevins

LOGLINE: A man-Slade Ripfire is the biggest baddass fordamn straight and other guys are all like, bring it and guess what?

ACT ONE: So Slade is loading his gun and his supervisors's all like: The criminals need rehabilitation and he shoots back-I've got 44 calibers of rehab six times here and the supervisor's all fag-face cause Slade just totally burns him.

Also the secretary's got big tits and she acts like a dyke but at the end she's fucking Slade.

CUT TO the park where this KluxKlan guy's beating on a black guy and all saying stuff like "Racist this and racist that" and then Slade's there saying :Why don't you fuck with the wrong motherfucker and come fuck with me

And we show the KluxKlan guy all putting up a cool and Slade shoots him so he's lifted off the ground in slow motion, but we show his head fly off and it's screaming while it's still flying.

Also, Slade is a black guy.

While Slade was killing the Klan guy there is a bank robbing: the twist-they were distracting Slade in the park while they took down the bank.

ACT TWO: Now there's been a rash of bank robs for two weeks and the supervisor won't listen to Slade.

'You stop these guys beating up minoritys in the parks' But it's a smokescreen-Slade and the supervisors just takes his badge and Slade's all like, 'Vietnam is all forgotten to you' and we show a picture: they were buddies in Vietnam.

The supervisors sits down on his one leg and is sad and is saying, 'You don't know the pressure I'm under and Slade's saying, 'Drive on, bro. And the supervisor: 'Just this once' and we see they are friends even though they yell everything.

ACT THREE: We're showing inside the bank and theres: 2 tellers a mom and 3 kids a guard an old woman and another guy.

Then all over the screen it's crash when a big motorcycle with sidecar comes through the front window – it's the robbers!

They machete the 2 kids and the old woman (with Slade's voice) says, 'Wrong move' and throws off his wig and purse – Slade was really the old lady.

Then for one hour he fucks up the robbers. The chief robber says, 'There's a minority getting beat on in the park:

197

FLASHBACK: Slade teaching every black guys kung-pow and now in the present the black guy is killing the robber's ass in the park-it was one of the black guys who learned kung-pow.

Slade: Now everyone minority is the wrong motherfucker to fuck with. And he karate kicks a stick of dynamite into the guys chest(first he shoots a hole so the dynamite will go in) The guy looks down and he's so fucked and Slade's all: 'Don't lose your head' This gets a big laugh because the guy's head dynamites off all the way to the ceiling (off the screen).

Then Slade fucks the secretary out of being a dyke.

Unseeable Fear

Treatment

By Erik Blevins

LOGLINE: Man's darkest night-mare of fear: a exorcist woman bitten by a man who's a Werewolf bitten by a vampire -and then turns invisible.

ACT ONE: Fog grips the night. An unholy howls in the air and we PAN INTO a house where evil dwells but looks normal (the house).

Close on a Bedroom where a woman in bed is screaming with a green-face and her eyes are just white. It's by a devil possessed and she's screaming "Fuck you fuck you faggot lick it my butt-hole" and it's the Devil making her say it.

'We've got to do something —her husband and the Priest is backing away scardedly from what we think is the bed and we REVEAL through the window a Wolf-Man in a cape is crashing through the glass.

The husband is totally No! Keep Away! – RAAAAAAAARGHHHHHHHH! Just completely going through him on the wall is blood from the husband and the priest crosses across his chest 'God perverse us' and the exorcist-woman says 'God sucks! ACCCCCCCCCHHHH she's being choked off by the wolf chewing her neck but she doesn't bleed because of the devil.

The Priest had a silver cross and the vampire inside the Wolf-man goes over the broken window and back out in the night. And he doesn't kill the exorcist-woman totally and she's a demon insider-her woman and also a vampire werewolf because the Wolf-man was bitten by a vampire earlier.

ACT TWO:

Now the husband has an eyepatch and fueled by vengeance 'The devil has hell to pay because it's personal on my part' he tells the room of scientists. They have a Weejee board wired to a future-computer, and they're tracking the possessing demon.

It's been five years thinks the husband and we can hear his thoughts and we realize he's been studying the occult and computers for five years straight and he's totally obssessed.

In the papers are piles of murders committed by an invisible wolf who bites his victims necks in the shape of a pentagram. The murders are sweeping the world and the populations is demanding they stop.

The president went to all the universities and top sites and put together the super-team the husband is leading now.

The board crackles to life and the computer smokes and explodes and on the screen it says, 'EVILOLIDON' the NAME OF THE DEMON!!

We're close on the husband's good eye and he's all focused and pissed off and the audience will be thinking: this is it.

ACT THREE:

The husband also got a female scientist to be in love with him but he's too obsessed and her love is unreturned. We hear the Heart song 'Alone' as she walks the city streets, thinking of the obsessed eyepatch husband, who's in Egypt fighting the demon.

Suddenly, she feels a headrush – her love is in trouble. A bunch of quick cuts together of her getting on an airplane to Egypt.

In Egypt at the Pyramid the husband is screaming, 'SHOW ME YOUR FACE!' and the demon Evilolidon rips him with a psychical claw which fells him and he can't go on, all the blood loss he's having. But the female scientist runs to the top of the pyramid and asserts her love for the eyepatch husband and the demon can't stand in the face of love and is banished. The husband and female scientist embrace – it was a battle of love versus evil.

MUSIC:

'You Can't Hurry Love" Phil Collins and also credits

TWIST EPILOGUE:

A janitor is sweeping up at the bottom of a cliff. His broom hits something invisible – it's the invisible

werewolf/vampire devil wife. She fell off a cliff earlier
in the movie when we were showing the husband and his
eyepatch.

Napoleon: Fighter of History

Treatment

By Erik Blevins

LOGLINE: Napoleon, the fighter of history –his life only told more bad-ass than you've ever read in a movie before.

ACT ONE; Napoleon is on the island of France and old-timey terrorists have taken it over., we demand a billion silver coin for the island and everyone's not doing anything they're so intimidated but Napoleon was in another room when they took it over, and he says, 'Let's do this and runs upstairs.

The terrorists need the access code for France and the France leader won't give it and the terrorist says, I will count to three (he does this in French with writing on the screen we can read) but the guy won't give it up and on three he blows the guy's head off.

Now Napoleon (who saw the leader get killed) is on the roof and tries calling the police and the fire department but they totally ignore him and then there's a sound on the stairs and it's a terrorist coming up to kill him.

They fight around all these power tools and Napoleon wins but the guys boots don't fit so he sends the dead-corpse down an elevator (old-timey, made of wood and rope) with writing on his chest 'NOW I HAVE A MUSKET HO HO HO' and the terrorist leader is trying to act all on top of it but he's shitting his old-timey pants (britches?)

ACT TWO: Now Napoleon is all in France's air shafts fucking with the terrorists they don't know what to do. At one point he throws a terrorists' body on a carriage and gets people involved and it all escalates. 'Yippie ki-ya motherfucker' says Napoleon at a crucial point where we know it's going to go down hard between he and the leader.

ACT THREE: Explosions and a tank and one of the terrorists hanging from a chain and all this other shooting on the roof and napoleon has a firehose wrapped around his middle dangling off the building.

Finally the terrorist has his wife backed against a window and napoleon has a musket taped to his back (he's got his shirt off but we'll make his French body-front not all flabby and filled with croissants and whipped cream) and he whips it out and totally shoots the guy – he falls in slow motion and France is saved.

He and his wife pull away – Veev French!

MUSIC: QUEEN "BOHEMIAN RHAPSODY"

Cancer Pond

Treatment

By Erik Blevins

LOGLINE: At a cabin near this pond (not called Cancer Pond) this old Grampaw guy gets dead from cancer and his family learns each not to be such assholes.

ACT ONE: This family where the DAD is stressed (by his family) and the MOM wanted to be a painter a long time ago but now her job is taking shit from Stressed Dad. Also the DAUGHTER wants to know about sex going in her and the SON plays baseball like a SISSY and also acts like a Sissy.

'Might as well go visit GRAMPAW' grumps the dad, paying a lot of bills. The MOM has baked some cookies and the DAD grabs the pan and throws it out onto the porch. 'Go ask the cookies, Marion, go ask the cookies' "Ask them what?' says the MOM. IF YOU DON'T KNOW YOU'RE A BIGGER DUMMIE THAN I THOUGHT' the daughter hears this and is running upstairs crying and the son is out swinging like a sissy and all the other kids call him fag and he tries some reefer.

The movie is set for drama as they pull up to Grampaw's Cabin.

ACT TWO: The DAD is on the phone the whole time at the cabin and Grampaw just wants to go fishing 'one more time' he says this is foreshadowing but the family misses it and the DAUGHTER meets this tractor-lawn guy and he's all sweaty with muscles peeking out where his chest-buttons are open on his shirt. They're all ready to fuck but the MOM gets in between it, not wanting the daughter to fuck while the whole Time wondering why she's not painting (note: the painting is a metaphor for her not fucking – the not painting = Not Fucking).

The SON is down at the lake trying to cast a pole and it's not working because he's such a sissy and GRAMPAW comes down with a big thick book 'what's that a book on fishing' you could say so says GRAMPAW and puts the book under his arm 'now try casting without dropping the book' the son tries a bunch of times and drops the book and some big boys in a rowboat call him a faggot. The son stomps off, getting called a fag, and doesn't see GRAMPAW cough up a fishtank full of blood.

ACT THREE: Now the Grampaw is all in bed coughing and wheezing and the MOM shoots a bird with a BB gun she's so frustrated (dead bird=no fucking)and the DAD is spending all his time at the bait shop where theres a fax (He's faxing in the woods which is a pschiatric sign of head troubles) and the DAUGHTER is all kissing on the tractor guy down in his crotch and the son is at the pond with the fishing pole he finally casts it just right and it's a moment of victory not only for fishing but he also hooks one of the mean kids eyes and pulls it out (audience

cheers). It's like bait on the hook and a trout bites it
and he runs home with is catch, leaving the mean kid all
bleedy-face and feeling put in his place and also his eye is
in a fish so double-burn.

Now the SON is in GRAMPAW'S bedroom with his fish
but he sees granpaw is all CANCER and dying and he
calls MOM and DAD and SIS in and in our final scene
they're all realizing how important life is and not to be so
wrapped up in bullshit (touching).

They symbolically eat the fish, and mom makes an
ornament out of the dead bird (a new artistic endevaor =
hope and possible fucking in the near future) and that's
what the credits are rolling over – the dead bird ornament
and it makes the audience think.

STAR WARS EPISODE I:

Laser Fire on a Robot Ship and also Boba Fett Already

STAR WARS EPISODE II:

Jar Jar Keeps Dying

STAR WARS EPISODE III:

Wookies Having a Gun Fight and a Hottie in a Metal Boner-Making Bikini

Treatment

By Erik Blevins

LOGLINE: a bertter version of the Star Wars movie and while they shpw it there's a picture in picture of George Lucas with the flu also getting butt-slammed.

ACT ONE: Kenobi Ken (younger with ponytail) is out practicing with his laserchopper. He's swooshing around and around, practising to be an old guy who helps Luke by dying.

Before this, though, in space:

YELLOW LETTERS FLOAT BY SAYING:

208

Star wars

Episode I

Laser Fire on a Robot Ship and also Boba Fett Already

A bunch of shit has gone down in space. Now everyone
thinks things are all cool and worked out but they aren't
by a long shot. Now evil forces have gathered together to
screw things up, and this will involve space ships zooming
around like bastards and also there will be a young, Boba
Fett in there with this other bad-ass bounty hunter, but
the second bounty hunter of course will be killed as you
didn't see him in the 4, 5 and 6.

On a planet in space, Obi Wan is practicing with his
laserchopper.

Okay, so that's what he's doing now. And he does a
mega-swoosh around his back and the laser chopper slips
through his fingers through the air.

The laser chopper goes through JarJar Binks, the frog-
homo from the swamp world. And he's going 'Me-sa
ooooooo pain hurting la la la'.

Obi-Wan had the laserchopper set on practice and it is
killing JarJar slowly, plus his frog-body is strange to the
chopper, and it's slowly sending hot laser energy through
his body —the pace of a snail and it's just now starting to
burn into his bones, feeling like if someone poured hot
popcorn grease into a zit you just popped.

Obi-Wan is going to pull the laser chopper out and then
Princess Natalie is there saying, 'Don't, you'll only kilkl
him twice as dead, we have to let it run it's course' and
Jar Jar is in no much pain he's screaming and so we pull
into his screaming mouth and then we

ARE IN SPACE :The dark of his mouth is now the
blackness of space and there's a big laser battle between
two ships – one ship looks like the Millem Falcon but no
plate on the top and no wookie inside – it's a young Lando
flying (he's a teenage black man) and there are two droid
ships like those duck droids from the first one? Chasing
him and he just blows them away like no problem.

Now the Emperor of Evil watches this from his in
space monster ship and he's shaking his head – we need
clones not droids and the audience will just totally shit
because this is the clone wars remember when Obi Wan or
someone said this in the fourth one we actually thought
was the first the first time we saw it when it first came
out?

Meanwhile Obi-wan and the Princess and R2 and
Golden-PO get on a ship to fight evil. They go to a Wookie
Planet where they see Chewbacca throwing bananas at
an Imperial Walker and someone says, 'That big walking
carpet will never fly a spaceship" and this will also get a
big laugh because, shit, I mean...CHEWBACCA.

ACT TWO: This whole act is Jar Jar back on the practice

planet just screaming and screaming as the lightsaber burns into him. Every inch of his bones is like a forest fire and now it is starting in on his muscles (melting them) skin (frying bacon) hair (turning them into baby wasps stinging, and also in pain –thewasps) and also in this scene a hot coffee droid will crash into him, and there will be hot coffee in his eyes

ACT THREE: Now there's a guy named Fred Fett on a planet of evil and earlier the emperor of Evil hired him to kill Goloden-PO so he wouldn't live to walk around with R2 (using his Jedi mind to change the future).

And Ben gets wind of the plan (mind-wind) and tracks down Fred Fett and they have a battle against good and evil. Ben battles him so hard afterward he has to change his name to Boba (big recongition from the audience) and puts a helmet on for shame. And now he hunts bounties. He hooks up with a second bounty hunter in this last act and they go back to the practice planet and hit Jar Jar with a board. The second bounty hunter is eaten by a sky-worm out of the sky. And Boba Fett shuts himself in all inside and becomes the cold-ass he is later.

Also, during this, Anakin Vader was o.s. turning into Darth Vader, and we see him in the last shot, leading into the sequel (Episode II).

END CREDITS SONG: "BUST A MOVE" YOUNG MC

Star Wars

Episode II

Jar Jar Keeps Dying

There's another crawl:

In this movie Jar Jar dies for two hours for being sucha
homofag.

And this whole movie is JarJar still slowly dying, and
at one point he's hit by a car which doesn't kill him but
looks fuckign cool when it throws him in the air.

MUSIC OVER END CREDITS: "Run to the Hills" Iron
Maiden

Star War

Episode III

Wookies Having a Gun Fight and a Hottie in a Boner-
Making Meta; Bikini

It opens with this crawl:

Now in the universe is the coming of the Empire and
also more spaceships and aliens that would fight but
eventually take down the empire but this isn't that tiem
now it a time ofr dark ass kicking and spaceships burning
and wookies punching peiople

ACT ONE: We open on Darth Vader but not in costume yet (Annakin) and he's acting all creepy and he's got the Stanley Kubrick face like you see in the Shining where he's staring at you from under hius forehad, and if you saw a guy like that on the street you'd call the police to taser him. His htotie wife is all like, "
What's wrong, annie?" and he just shakes his head and says nothing. We know its because The Dark Fofce is taking him over but she doesn't know and goes back to makinbg breakfast.

Meanwhile the stormtroopers are forming their own metal planet (foreshadowing – the Death Star) and all of the goood people are being pout on a different planet where they get pounched all day. Things are looking bad so Obi-Wan and R22 and Golden-Po go to a planet of Other Jedis to form an army to take down the stormtroopers and also the old Robe Guy. And they're counting on Anakin to help them and he acts all helpful but really he's going to put ona helmet and kill everyone.

ACT TWO: Obi Wan realizes they need the help of the Wookies so he goes to the planet of Wookies where they use Ewoks as tampons. Obi Wan reveals he knows Wookie language and he helps them to swing in the trees and at one point he's challenged to a coconut throwing contest and he wins so he wins over the wookies. And we reveal one of them is Chewbacca, and the audsicne des a double shit.

ACT THREE: We just show the ROAD WARRIOR and that scene in DANGEROUS LISIOSNS where Uma gets boobs out.

SONG: "Ghostbusters" theme

Baby Grandmas

Treatment

By Erik Blevins

LOGLINE: Hilarity changes its name to hi-fucking-larity because of the hijinks that are packed into this hilarious script: hijinks+hilarious equals the word "fucking" in there between the hilarity-word.

ACT ONE: At a TOP SECRET labrotory of research in the secret hills a SCIENTIST Woman is adding different colored fluids to bottles as she experiments. "This will be my greatest creation' she says a way to reverse the aging process so that as people gorw into grandma and prandpa age they actualkly turn into babies and start the process all over again. That way as they grow older they'll know to work out a lot and be supermen when they're twenty. And also there will be a part of the potion I'll add that will make it so I can conmtrol them when they're at superman stage.

In the town below the laboratrory, two Grandmas are fighting over who gets more attention from their granddaughter (the granddaughter is a baby) They're doing all these funny bits (to look at – the audience)

215

where they each buy a bigger and better toy for the
granddaughter and they're competing back and forth.
At one point they cause a car accident which actually
involves a garbage and ice cream truck (separate) and
a goldfish store it crashes into – both the trucks. The
granddaughter laughs when she sees the accident. The
grandmas are both exasperated in their face at the way
they compete on each other.

"If only we could remember what it was like to be a
granddaughter" says the grandmas, each thinking they if
they could they could be the best grandma.

ACT TWO: The Scientist Woman is almost done with her
formula and she has a trained oranga-monkey to help her
out in the laboratory (wearing a tuxedo). The oranag-
monkey grabs the formula and runs out of the laboratory,
and the Scientist Woman tries to stop it, but it is to no
avail. "I've got to get that formula back".

Meanwhile, we have a MONTAGE (CUT-TOGETHER)
of the monkey-chimp making his way to town with the
formula. He jumps into a tree, down onto the ground,
runs along the road, fightens a car-driver (into a tree –
dead) hitches a ride on the back of a lettuce truck (into
town) throws a ball of lettuce at a hitchhiker, jumps off
the truck into the town center, brings mayhem to some
Girl Scouts having a outdoor day and farts on a window-
washer. The window washer drops his window-liquid
bottle on the groudn – the spray-top flies off and at the

216

same time the runaway monk-achimp drops the formula
onto the ground where it bounces (the formula part) out
of the formula jar and into the window washing water and
then the spary-top comes back onto the bottle. *Note: Now
the window-washer bottle has the formula in it.

Meanwhile the two grandmas are still trying to impress
the granddaughter-baby and they start up on the hi-jinks
again by drinking funny things in front of the baby
(old ladies drinking things they shouldn't not drink =
huge laughs) and then one of the grandmas just grabs
the window-washing water and drinks it and the other
grandma (thinking: she's going to beat it over me drinking
the washing-water) and so she grabs the water and drinks
and then in a moment they're obth babies – only they're
actually BABY GRANDMAS.

ACT THREE: Just a whole lot of funny shit at once with
the Lady Scientist falling into a pool and the monkey
drives a steam roller and chases the mayor and the baby
grandmas form a rap group with their granddaughter and
there's also a treasure that the two grandmas use to buy
them each their own granddaughter (after they turn back
all oldy like real grandmas).

END CREDITS MUSIC: Bobby Brown "My Prerogative"

Carvin' It U!p 2 Da Streetz

Treatment by

Erik Blevins

LOGLINE: This urban high school (hip hop and also fighting in the students) geta a new teacher and he brings hope and also he's no-nonsense and everyone learns including him. AWESOME SOUNDTRACK.

ACT ONE: So we track through ths high school everything fgoing wrong and the kids are all heade for total cirm (spraypaiitng and rape and drugs and punching people and breakdaincing in the night) and we see teachers trying to get their kids to read and the kids are all: The fuck do we need to read for boyeeee and when the teacher isn't looking they write FART and BOOKS SUX on the blackboard and this one teacher jumps out the window she's so scared.

The Principle is in his office and he's rubbing the top of his head with both hands (=tension and we know he's at a breaking point which the audience wil know somehting's going to turn around() and his assiatant is saying. You know what we gotta do" and the Principle is saying "But

218

we can't you remmebr the last time" and the assiattnt is
But we have to and the Pirnciple is saying "but it's too
risky and the assiatant is all like "it's our only hope" and
the principle is like There's got ot be a better way and
th assiattn is like "We tried everything else and then the
priunciple is saying "it's my repiuyation on the line

(Importsnt note: Each time we'll be closer and coser on
the Principle and the assiattns' face = DRAMA)

And the Principel is about to say "he's a loose cannon
and then a teacher gets thronw through the wall by these
three thug kids (MURDER-BIZ, Biz-Murder and Murder)
and the teacher' head comes off and the assiatsnt raises
his eyebrows at the Principle like he;s saying See? And
the principle nods his head okay without saying anything
he's so defeated.

MUSIC: Go Go's Head Over Heels (about the teacher's
head falling off)

ACT TWO: We're looking up atht eh high school form the
ground, ike the camers is on the ground? It's this low
angle and kids are messing around then, from the left side
of the screne this motorcycle comes rolls up and a boot
his the ground with a bandana tied around it and in their
heads the audience is going to hear George Thorogood's
"Bad to the Bone" and then we FREAK THEIR SHIT OUT
qwhen hat actual song plays.

And we follow the boot and it's waling into the school (and
we'll also film upwatrds to see the boto is attchaed to this
badss dude) and the kida re all laughing and pointing and
one of them pees on the guy buy the guy doesn't even
react. He just turns and saysn. You owe me one pair of
Gap jeans" and keeps going and the other kids are like burn!

Then we're in the prtinciple's office where he's meeting
with the badass dude and the badass dude says "good to
see you again" like nothing badass is about to hapena dn
the principle is throwing up from tension and says, "just
teach the kids, let's not have another Sideweat High School
on our hands and he badass dude says "Last I checked,
Sidewesst High had scores of all 100 across the coard
and the principel says But AT WHAT COST and the badass
dude says You can afford it and then Bad to the Bone
again as he leaves.

And the assitant principle meets him in the hallway and
says (like he's joking with a buddy) Mr. Tuffteach! And the
badass dude says that's wht the students are going ot call
me. It's chet to you and the assistant says Whatever Chet,
just don't break out balls too much and then they see a
student spraypaint nine penuses on a picture of George
Washington and Tuffteach says, :ooks like they're already
broken and the assistant makes a I'm Burned Face and
Tuffteach heads off to class.

ACT TWO: Tuffteach goes into the classroom and the
kids and burning a desk and peeing on it and he doesn't

even react he's such a badass. He goes to the board and
everyone stops because uslaly the teacher goes crazy wen
he sees fire and peeing but Tuffteach just writes his name
on the blackboard and it says MR. TUFFTEACH and all the
students crack up.

You aint for real! Says one and another one says Aw
hell NAW AND A THIRD ONE says Aw shit. (NOTE: All
the students are black students except for the ones who
are Mexican and white and females of different colors)

Then one of the students takes out a gun and aims it
sideways really coll and he shotos at Tuffteach. And
before the bullets can get to him Tuffteach holds up...

...a PUMPKIN, which he uses to absorb the bullets. The
pumpkins almost breaks apart, but Tufteach kind of
hold sit togther. The students are all like no way, and
then they shit with their eyes when Tuffteach turns
the pumpkins arpund. The bullet have smacked intot
he other side, and we see a very basic, kinda beginners
type jack o lantern – only it was the bullets that sort of
punched throguht eheyes nose and mouth.

Then Tuffteach says, "Class is in session" and fuck yeah
here comes Bad to the bone again.

Then through he door ot eh clsssrom come this hot
Science TEahcer form next door Terersa Buinsen and she's
got boob cleavage which is what we film first before we

swoop up toi her hot face and she says "uh, I guess your
new here but we try to not have the students shoot during
class only sfter class and then Tuffteach looks over his
shoulder at her and says "the only gun you'll hear going
off around here from now on will be mine. And the classe
goes oooweeeee ;cu theyr'e thinking when he says gun it
means his dick and when he says going off it means its
ging into Mrs. Bunsen's lap when there's a R. Kelly sogn
playing.

Mrs Bunsen doesn't know what to say and she makes that
kind fo face where you know she and tuffteach are gong to
mak be making it all happen later but right now we odn't
know how that going to happen to supoer-sex-suspence.

Then through the door come Murder-Biz, Biz-Murder and
Murder (*note we hould get rappers cause they can do
sogns on the movie and then sell the movie songs). They
stare atTuffteach and he stares back and then Biz-Murder
goes: You don't want to be staring like that and Tuffteach
says you mean like the way you shouldn't be staring at
me? And the class literally shits their pants and then Biz-
Murder says Later and turns to his dudes and says Let's
bust out of here (which is a black epression) and they
leve the classroom. Tuffteach says I'll sauve some
seats for you, nd we know this is going to be his biggest
challenge.

Then Tuffteach says Get out your class books and the
students are all like, What about the pumpkins? And

tuffteach says you're going to find out about that if you
stay after school in the gy where I have a special program
and the kids are all like We ain't staying after no fucking
school nd Tuffteach just smiles and we know something's
totally up.

Then we cut to the gymnasium and it's after school and
Mr. Tuffteach is standing there with all these things (we
can't see what they're yet) but they're covered with
towels and there's fifteen of them. Up in the bealchers,
Mrs. Busen is watchignh im meaningingfully (=she wants
to make sex on him) but she hide swhen he looks uop (he
senses her; the sex fumes).

Then TWELVE od the students come into the gymnasium
and see Tuffteach standing there and they come over – we
go to a cool slow motion shot of them waling forward and
whatever is the top rap song in the USA should paly over
them wlking uo to Mr, Tufftach.

"What' this stupid-ass thing anway?' asks one of the kids
because they have to act like ti's stupid vause that;s hwo
your cool.,

then mr tufftcach takco off all tho towolo at tho
same time, adnw e see theyr'e pumpkins HOLY SHIT
PUMPKINS?!?   What's going on?

So then one of the students says, "Pumpkins holy shit
PUMPKINS HWt's going on?"

And Mr, tuffteach says Pumpkin carving ever heard of it?

Yeah, we got Halloween and shit down here (this is one
of the girls who'll get pregnant later but for now it's a
surprise) so what?

Did you know winning apumpokin carving competition can
get oyuu college credit?

Man, you crazy? Crazy or loco says Mr. Tuffteach? And
all the students reep[ect him a little more.

Hey there's three etra pimpkins sayd the Get Pregnant
Later Girl, and Mr. Tuffteach says, Oh Really? And they
all look over and there's
Murder-Biz, Biz Murder and Murder.

Nice to see you, Murder-Biz. Grab a knife says Tuffteach.

ACT TWO: Los of scenes strung together (French word)
of the kids leanring to carve pumpkins. We get fiunny
stuff like one kid cuts a hole too big in the top and the
lid falls through, and then another kid carves FUCK inhis
pumpkins and another kid cuts off thre fingers.

MUSIC: Something by Public Enemy when they sing about
punching people

Then suddenly we're at a teachers board meeting where
they're all saying to Mr. Tuffteach – we don't have all this

extra money for pumpkisn and he's all These kids can
get pumpkin carving college credit and we see how Mrs.
Bunsen is trying to be practical but also her sex wants to
be all on top of Mr Tuffteach.

Then Mr. tufftach is back with the kids, and he's
making them cavre perfect triangles for eyes and another
perfect triangle for a nose and a perfect half circle fo r
amouth and lot letting them be creative and bring "da
streetz" to the punpkin carving.

And suddenly its their first competition with another high
scjool and they get beaten. And now the kids are in crisis:

The Get Preegnent girl gets pregnant

Another kid starts doig crack

Another kid drops out of school all together

Biz-Murde,r Murder-Biz and Murder murder people.

The school's going to cut their funding altogether and
TuffTeach;'s packing his stuff and suddenly Mrs. Bunsen
gots all up in afoos about You tought those kids to carve
out a better life and now you're leaving your life punpkin
with a frowny face. It's a speech that's about life
but also shows how pumpkin carving it about life and
Tuffteach suddenly realizes that and he's al "Let's do this"
and GEORGE THOROGOOD AGAIN.

ACT THREE: So now he's got to round up the kids and
set them straight so he get the one kid off of crack and
the other one to not drop out of school and helps Biz-
Murder, Murder-Biz and Murder dump all the dead bodies
into a woodchipper so now all the kids know he cares.

So then they go to a pumpkin patch in the middle of ht
ecity and steal a bunch of pumpkins and they're back I
the auditiroum, and the Now Pregnant Girl comes in.   Her
belly is really big and we're thinking she's coming to say
goodbye except then she lifts her shirt and she;s drawn
a jack o lantern fce on her stomach.   "I'm gonna name
him jack."   And everyone laughs and Mr. Tufftech says,
"I thought we were gonna carve some pumpkins" and
everyone goes yeah and GEORGE THROROGOOD and:

Now the kids ar eusing their street skilsl to carve the
pumpkins.   One kid spins on his back and balances a
pumpkin on his feet hwile another kid carves it.   Biz-
Murder, Murder-Biz and Murder shoot facesinto the
pumpkisn with guns held sideways looking cool and then
when they turn the pumpkins around they look like the
Sistine Chapel.

Then it's time for the big final showdown with the top
pumpkin carving high school and it should be filmed like
DRUMLINE and THUNDERDOME and also SMOKEY AND
THE BANDIT.

So while this awesome rap song plays the team is totally kicking ass and Mrs. Bunsen has this look like she's totally going to fuck Tuffteach and the principle is getting out his checkbook formore pumpkin carving and the pregnant girl gives birth but still manages to finisha pumpkin that we realize is a baby crib which she puts her baby in and Biz-Murder has three seconds left to finish his pumpkin and with one bullet he shoots Malcolm X's face into the pumpkin and the team wins.

Then an old man in a farmer suit comes into the auditorium – it's Biz-Murder's dad who was always a pumpkin farmer only he and his dad never got alogn but now they hug and everyone jumps in the air and FREEZE FRAME

T-Pain (not written yet): Pump That Kin the Fuck Up!

PUSSYPUP AND ROVER-KITTY:

The Mixed-Up Dog and Cat

Treatment

By Erik Blevins

LOGLINE: A cat and a dog switch brains back and forth so now there's a cat thinks I'm a dog and a dog with a cat-brain in his head -for all ages.

ACT ONE: There's a moving truck on a quiet street it's the suburbs and the Flawson Family is moving into their address. Their daughter is Kit and she's unpacking her street hockey gear.

All of a sudden, from next door, we look over and there's the son of the family next door Bruce Slingerland and his street hockey team. They're the Ice Dragons the coolest team of slicks to ever skate the streets that's what Bruce says to her and she's all, wait until you see a thing or two. They just laugh and she turns to her sister.

'They don't look so hot' only it comes out as if she didn't make an L sound a D sound a S sound a H sound her sister is deaf and never learned normal talk. You sure got that right sis Kit is saying and her dog Rover and her cat Pussy woof and cat-meow in agreement. It's

228

like the animals are agreeing with her which they don't actually do and this gets a laugh.

NOTE: The father will be falling down the truck ramp in the background, with

MUSIC: Bump – a –booooowwww to show us he's funny this WHOLE FIRST PART.

ACT TWO: The Ice Dragons are tearing up the street playing hockey in the cul-de-sac of the neighborhood where their house and the Flawsons are. There's a spooky old house in the cul-de-sac at the end part and every now and then they are glancing at it pretending to be slicks but it's spooky in the afternoon.

Then Kit and her sister and Rover and Pussy are on the scene, Kit in her gear and her sister not hearing anything. And the Ice Dragons totally snob her NO GIRLS ALLOWED they all chant and Kit says, What's it take to get on your team?

Bruce their team captain starts to say something and then Freckles McGee says –Hold up, there's a way and points to the spooky old cul-de-sac house. Knock on the door and see who answers, then we'll think about it.

And before they can say anything Kit's up at the door knock knock knock and the door opens:

THE POINT OF VIEW INSIDE: An old gypsy woman opens the door it's Madame Witchcraft, and she's in the middle of a spell –"Switchery witchery hoog-a da hooooo..." But she opens the door and is scared by a girl in hockey clothes and drops her crystal ball. It rolls across the lawn, and Rover and Pussy both take a sniff.

BZZZZAP! The ball explodes, and Rover and Pussy do a mid-air flip.

Oh no, the Spell of switchery! Cries Madame Witchcraft, and slams the door.

The Ice Dragons are all freaked out – they tear out of there doing Warp Factor 9000!! You bunch of sissies! Yells Kit. Her sister is pointing and making weird vowel-words only it doesn't freak out Kit because she's used to it her whole life. Her sister is pointing at the pets, which are now coming to : except Rover is meowing and Pussy is messing on a fire hydrant!

ACT THREE: MONTAGE: (SONG, "WHAT'S NEW, PUSSYCAT?" TOM JONES) Rover is playing with yarn: Pussy is chasing other cats; Rover in a litter-box; Pussy is eating dog food; Rover is chasing mice; Pussy is chasing the mailman; Rover is cleaning himself like a cat **THIS WILL BE HILARIOUS**

Kit is upset – My pets are mixed up, and there's no one to play street hockey with. There will be a killer scene here for the trailer where the sister tries to act out that they have to go to Madame Witchcraft only Kit's not getting it and then finally she'll say We have to go to Madame Witchcraft as if she thought it up and the sister will roll her eyes (this will be a special effect, since deaf people can't actually do this).

AT MADAME WITCHCRAFT'S PLACE: My dog and cat are driving me crazy. I mean my cat and dog. I mean, I don't know what I mean. They're all switched up! It's like they're Pussypup and Rover-Kitty (very ironical: see TITLE) Kit is saying all of this.

Madame Witchcraft is looking into her crystal ball (repaired) You have to defeat the Ice Dragons in the big street hockey finals. But I don't have a team! It's the only way, says Madame Witchcraft. Now leave here.

Kit is in her front yard, in the dumps. She looks over and sees Rover cough up a hairball. I'll do it she thinks.

MONTAGE (SONG, ANYTHING BY GLASS TIGER) Kit trains her sister and a fat kid on the block and a wheelchair kid and a scabies kid to play street hockey (we'll show earlier the Ice Dragons being mean to these other kids: chasing the fat kid into a heat-stroke, giving the wheelchair kid lemonade that gives you the runs, throwing ants on the scabies kid).

The day of the big game and the Ice Dragons are doing well but then Kit's strategy becomes clear. Her sister can't hear their trash-talking, and the fat kid is a good goalie (wide) and the wheelchair kid is now super-motorized (we'll show that Kit's dad is a clumsy inventor also) and the scabies kid's dad is Wayne Gretsky (cameo).

And Kit's team wins the championship and Bruce is their friend now and Kit sees that Rover and Pussy are back to normal – only they turned back days before, and we show Madame Witchcraft smiling and then

CUT TO: MADAME WITCHCRAFT'S BASEMENT there's her street hookey clothes from when she was a little girl she was inspiring Kit the whole time.

LAST SHOT: The scabies kid and the wheelchair kid are both about to touch the crystal ball. THE END???????

SLADE RIPFIRE:

Burning Explosion of Hell-Flame and Justice

Treatment

By Erik Blevins

LOGLINE: Jesus living fuck-nuts. Seriously.

ACT ONE: It's "August-pimp month in the city – Slade thinks on the roof where we show him looking at the city from a helicopter (he's not in a helicopter but the audience is swooping around him and he's doing big brooding letting you know some foot-to-ass shit's coming down. These pimp days are going to go to the dogs this time, he thinks, not so we can hear him but you'll know the way he's gripping his gun and has an overcoat on with no shirt and boots with the pants tucked in.

Suddenly, below him: the scream of a prostiwhore getting a razor party on her face and the sun's also going down at the same time and Slade jumps off the roof, shooting his blastiMagnum so hard at the ground it slows his fall enough so he lets down featherfoot right next to this killer pimp going slash-ass on this hot chick.

And Slade's like 'I guess you think you own the city and the pimp's all like 'it's just one big whore and Slade goes this whore wears a dress made of justice and the audience

232

sees the whore he's talking about is really him he was
doing a word-flip on the pimp to coNfuse him into letting
bullets go in his tummy.

The bullets take the tummy out his back and onto a
wall soelling out the titles, The whore thanks him and we
see Slade's in love-she's looking all "chili-mac Face" but he
loves what's inside and

NOTE: Message for the audience teaching them
importance.

ACT TWO: Now the Pimps of the city have a clubhouse
where they all agree to kill Sladebut first 'we'll humiliate
him to the ground, bringing him downlow for everyone to
see

And this one pimp shows this tiny dress they plan to
put on Slade and chase him through the park throwing
firecrackers.

Now the trap is set and also they kidnap the burned-up
Muppet-faced hooker Slade loves deep inside and tie her to
a rocket made of suede.

On the Tv 'This is a message to Slade Ripfire' we have
your love tied to our rocket and it's pointed straight at
City Hall where they keep the explosives and if you want
to see her pretty face again and not all over the streets
(gets a laugh because if the rocket blows up her face will
be spread all over the place but now in one piece hence;
-ON THE STREETS -also she's not pretty) you put on this
dress and run from firecrackers we throw at you in the
park

THE MAYOR and THE PRESIDENT and an IMPORTANT

Guy order Slade to put on the dress and Slade throws his
badge off the Lincoln Memorial (irony: Slade's a black guy
black guy=Lincoln statue) and now it's personal.

ACT THREE: Now Slade looks like he is giving up to the
pimps. He meets with them all at once and bends down
like saying –go ahead, let's get into the dress and the
pimps come forward and then Slade suddenly stands up –
   BIG TWIST – Slade has a gun UNDER His jacket. HUGE
SURPRISE for the audience and then CHEERING
   Because Slade just lets go shooting at all the pimps.
   Note: We can have them die in all these funny pimp
ways. Like he shoots through one guy's wide-brimmed hat
and the brains shoot out onto the brim and just sit there.
Or another guy the bullets rochcets off all his rings and
he's all thinking he's safe and he walks around the corner
and the bullet gets him then.
   The LEADER Pimp and Slade have a karate-punch battle
(Slade is out of bullets and also the sword in the pimp's
cane Slade uses to kill another pimp) until Slade punches
him and he falls back on the controls, laucnhing the
rocket. In the two seconds before it launches Slade unties
the LiteBrite face hooker and ties the LEADER Pimp to it
and the rocket takes off, destroying City Hall in a
   BURNING EXPLOSION OF HELL-FLAME AND
JUSTICE!!!!!!

   EPI-ENDING; You blew up City Hall – and for what'?
this is his supervisor.

Slade looks at the NuttyBuddyface Hooker and says, 'Let's just say I learned something about looking on the inside and not in the scrungly-part of a fucked-up hooker face." And the audience applauds.

SLADE RIPFIRE:
Deadly Blood-Kick to Oblivion

Treatment

By Erik Blevins

LOGLINE: It's a crime movie of so much action it can't be wrote about without MOTHERFUCKER and OH FUCKING YEAH and FUCK-YEAH in capitol letters in the logline, it's that whomping bad-ass get ready.

ACT ONE: All over the city there are karate crimes of deadly portions where it's clear a karate expert was doing the crime.

We show close of a man's face where it's totally kicked inside out, and then pull-up to show Slade Ripfire, looking over the crime scene of eighty bodies on the street and a fire hydrant broken and cars crashed and he's telling the supervisor 'Whoever is doing this is just getting warmed up.'

I don't want anymore of your lone-cannon methods on this getting everything bloody' says the supervisor

And Slade says, 'Better him than me' And the supervisor's all pale in the head because he knows Slade's going to turn it on.

Meanwhile, in an alleyway, A Mystery-Guy watches Slade from the shadows.

ACT TWO: Now Slade is looking at a bunch of evidence material in MONTAGE: a eyeball at a bank, a ripped-out spine hanging from a tree in front of a gold-deposit, jewelry store filled with guts (stomped on).

Outside the jewelry store someone guns at him and Slade ducks as a hole is in the wall –lets rock the HOUSE! And he's got his gun out.

Slade can't tell where the bullets are coming from until a priest a little girl her dog a woman with a bag of fish all four goldfish in the bag a businessman a ice cream truck man a mailman a guitar man on the street a mime another woman three other kids an important man with a case a family of eight a chinese guy (one) three cops a rollerskate girl are all mowed down by the rain of bullets and Slade traces it over to a building across the street and he bolts for it.

Inside the building the killer is pounding up the stairs and Slade THROWS HIS GUN up the stairs going upstairs it hits the ceiling and goes off, gunning the killer in the chest where we see Slade running up the stairs through the new big hole in the guys chest (WE FILM THROUGH THE HOLE).

Slade is over the killer, shaking and going Who sent you motherfucker? And the killer is about to say a name where a foot comes from off-camera we didn't see before and punches the killer's face clean off before he can respond. Slade looks up

-long time no see. And now with that tension we're on to

ACT THREE: The killer revealed – it's Cho-Cho Washington, the baddest black-chicano karate teach in the city (Slade is all black with no chicano).

'Turning to crime like a bitch says Slade, fisting up and getting all posed for fighting. 'I'm going to turn you back an by back I mean all the way off

'Join me and we'll have this city under our feet

'I'm gonna have your balls under my feet with your ass around my feet from sticking my foot up it' says Slade, and moves on him

Cho-Cho aims a kick that goes through the wall as Slade ducks, and he realizes —Cho-Cho is versed in the Deadly Blood-Kick to Oblivion, the deadliest move in karate-fighting.

Slade has a challenge. They fight up and down the stairs, slade at one point throwing Cho-Cho eighty flights down but Cho-Cho pops up as Slade walks down the stairs to leave the building (we think the movie is over) and fights even though his neckbone sticks out.

Finally, Slade is down for the count and Cho-Cho aims the Deadly Blood-Kick to Oblivion right at Slade's head and Slade takes the plastic explosive in his boot heel and jams it between Cho-Cho's toes in an ultimate defense move.

'Try and learn some devil-foo in Hell' 'I'll be waiting to use it on you' says Cho-Cho, even though his foot's about to explode he keeps a rock-face because he's such a bad ass and Slade totally blows him to parts all over the stairs.

Three women that'll be in the movie earlier are on the roof. Slade rescues them and they fuck over the credits.

Appendix B:
Neill Cumpston

Years after I created Erik Blevins, I created Neill Cumpston.

I'd been invited to an early screening of *Blade II* at Mann's Chinese Theater. I was friends with some of the AintItCoolNews guys, and when I told them I was going, one of them said, "Hey, write up a review and we'll run it."

Blade II ended up being a pretty terrific movie—even better than *Blade,* and that's saying something. Guillermo del Toro managed to inject the movie with as much enthusiasm as he did pathos, and David Goyer's script was smart without being smart-alecky. I remember being excited to the point of giddy when I left—which is the way I want to feel after a good action flick. The only bad movies are boring ones.

But I made the mistake, when I started writing my review, of trying to give a serious assessment of the film itself. It read like someone telling you they'd enjoyed the film instead of showing you how they enjoyed the film.

Some of the reviews on AintItCool—especially the ones by random viewers and fans who've gotten into an early screening—are exhilarating reads. In their nonsensical, lapel-pawing enthusiasm lies the truest expression of the thrill-splash that the light, noise, and movement of movies give to their audiences.

I realized I wanted to re-create that in the review, and Neill Cumpston was born.

Neill ended up having way more of a life outside his ersatz existence than Erik Blevins ever did. Peter Travers quoted the opening paragraph of Neill's *X-Men 2* review in *Rolling Stone*. Howard Stern read the *Matrix Reloaded* review on his show. And certain other filmmakers, once they begged Neill's identity from the AintItCool guys, began inviting me to their screenings, wanting their own Cumpston reviews.

I realized though, with the *Spider-Man 3* review—once I'd created an extended family history for Neill—that the character had quickly run his course. I've written other reviews for AintItCool, but always under my name and in my voice. I don't want to do character anymore. Unless I'm acting.

Enjoy Neill. He could not be more excited to meet you, as you'll see.

BLADE FUCKIN' II! FUCK YEAH!

Man, like I just came from seeing *Blade Fuckin II* and I'm writing the title like that because aw man you're going to be so blown away you'll be all like, *"Blade Fuckin II,* that's what it should be called not *Blade II* because seriously HOLY SHIT."* Even if you're talking to your grandparents visiting from Ohio you'll have like F-words flying because the movie kicks ass with a boot made of burning meat.

Also, if you see it with your girlfriend you'll automatically break up because hey, chicks stay away from this one. Go see *Wedding Planner* or that other one with the British guy and the bookstore and the cute dog and the herbal tea because this movie isn't for the chicks. Maybe for the chicks who ride motorcycles and can beat up pit bulls, maybe, but like holy shit fuckin boom! Pow bang yeah!

The movie is all about vampires which are bad enough but then there's these other vampires which are all like worse—their mouths are like garbage disposals so when they bite someone it's like a log flume ride made of blood and also there's heavy metal music playing over it.

The other vampires—the disposal mouth dudes are eating up the regular vampires so they're all like, "We gotta get Blade to help us" so they totally get him to go in with this group of ass-kicking vampires and here's the twist—they were trained to kill Blade only

now they and Blade have to work together to kill the super-vamps
and then, from that point on (MAJOR SPOILERS AHEAD):

FUCKING SLASH KICK GUNS HEADS BLOWN OFF GODDAMN
MOTORCYCLE FIGHT SCENES PUNCHING EYEBALLS
OUT FLYING GUTS THROUGH THE AIR AND ALSO THIS
ONE TOTALLY HOT CHICK SPURT CRUSH SNAP BONES
EXPLOSIONS FIRE MELT-Y EXPLOSIONS SLAUGHTER
MASSACRE RUN JUMP FLIP OVER HAMMER MACHINE GUN
THROWING KNIFE-Y THING DEAD.

So when someone tells you this movie doesn't totally kick ass it's
legal for you to break a bottle over their head and kick them in the
groin and you can also fight the cops who show up to take you
away—the movie is that bad-ass. See it before everyone thinks
you're gay.

Neill Cumpston
3/21/02

X2: X-MEN KICKING YOU IN THE BALLS SO HARD THAT YOU PUKE ON YOUR BALLS AND ALSO YOUR ASS

I know this movie has another title but that's what it should be called 'cause this movie kicks balls/ass/both. THANK FUCK THE OSCARS ARE OVER! Bunch of films going, "Ewwh, please don't hit me I'm so delicate and I'm made out of flower petals and also give me a reward." And now this is the first one coming along going, "Get ready to have your balls kicked" and before you can say, "What'd you say?" it kicks you in the balls and eats out your girlfriend.

This one's got Hannibal Lecter from the Manhunter of the Lambs film only now he's this government bad-ass and he's all, "I'm taking out the mutants" and holy shit he's serious, 'cuz you see him making all these mutants do evil shit, and meanwhile the good mutants at the Good Mutants School have to stop him, and they're forced to team up with the evil mutants. So we get to see Rogue (hottie) and this Ice Dude (gay-looking, but Rogue seems to want to fuck him so what do I know?) and this Fire Kid who's all three steps from going Columbine every second of his life and that boring Cyclops dick and showing-her-boobs-for-an-Oscar Storm and Mind Control Redhead and Wheelchair Charlie and finally Fuck Yeah Wolverine (which should be his official name) having to hook it up with Magnet-Gandalf and Rebecca Romijn-Nudeass to take out the evil government dude. Whooba-dow!

243

Remember how the first film had all that Story (= for gays) in the first part, and you were like, "How 'bout some ass-kicking already?" and then finally they got to it? Not this one. It's like okay, there's the credits, and now here's the ass-kicking and it starts and doesn't stop and you're all like, "Pants, meet shit."

MINOR SPOILERS:

There's this new blue Christian German mutant called Nightcrawler that can zap in and out of existence, and at first you think he's evil but then you find out the government dude was just controlling him. He almost kills the fucking president, and he's all about to stab him but then he's stopped and the audience is all bummed out, 'cause stabbing a president = cool flick. Also, you see Wolverine naked for a few seconds and that blue chick naked a lot (not TECHNICALLY naked but it's so easy to jerk off to her later when the DVD comes out).

MEDIUM SPOILERS:

There's also a mutant called Hottie Asian, I think, but she's got claws like Wolverine, and we find out where Wolverine got his claws, and they have a fight and the way Wolverine beats her you're like, "That sort of sucks 'cause I'd like to see her back" but sometimes cool characters gets Darth Mauled but that's the breaks.

MAJOR SPOILERS:

Mind Control Redhead dies. Wolverine and Mystique almost make out. I shitted my pants during an explosion scene.

244

Okay, that's it. I'm good until MATRIX 2: KINGDOM OF ASS-KICKING and HULK-MAN and I think there's something coming out with a werewolf in it.

Neill Cumpston
4/22/03

MATRIX: KINGDOM OF ASS-KICKING

Jim-Jammity Jesus Krispy Kreme Christ on a twat-rocket, this movie blew me apart and put me back together only after I'd got put back I felt like I had thirteen dicks and they'd all gotten blown by a surfer chick with 26 heads (2 mouths on each cock). I will see it ten times and if I see Star Wars George or that gay Batman director butt-hole any time during the ten screenings here comes Mr. Punch.

This is the sequel to the MATRIX Movie that came out four years ago and after seeing it I can say I could have waited another four years it is that fucking good. This movie is a pillowcase with soda cans inside that beats the living mule-fuck out of you but you're all like, "Bring it on honky tonk" because the beating feels like summer and Halloween and Cheetos at the same time. This movie is Mad Max's shotgun-gun from ROAD WARRIOR, only it shoots ass-kicking only at jocks. This movie is tits!

WARNING: THIS PARAGRAPH IS ABOUT THE PLOT AND IT'S BORING AND THERE'S NO ASS-KICKING IN IT BUT I USE THE WORD "FUCK" THREE TIMES TO HELP GET THROUGH IT

I still don't get the plot of the first one, and this one's all talking about "choices" (over and over again to where you think you're watching that fucking Chicktime network) and "prophecies" and especially words like "anomaly" and "exile" (and who the fuck even knows what those words mean?) and there's this long speech at the end that I also didn't get. Also, you find out all this deep stuff, like about The Cookie Lady from the first movie and they introduce all these other characters like a Key Guy and a Frenchie Dude and another Frenchie but guess what it's okay 'cuz the other Frenchie's a chick and she's got cleavage you could hide a rump roast in and also this ex-girlfriend of Murphus and there's this new guy on the ship flying it around, I think he's from OZ (don't worry, no butt rape). And Neo and Memento Babe are all PDA every second, and they also "do it" and one time I thought I saw Memento Babe's nip but it was one of those metal ring things that everyone's got on 'em so no jacking off when the DVD comes out.

So that's the plot but here's the thing: you could wear headphones and listen to Dio during this whole movie and you wouldn't miss anything, there's so much ass-kicking going on. That Smith Dude is back, only now he can make more Smith Dudes and do they each know how to kick ass? Like a Heroclix collector knows how to not get pussy. Plus he's got this other ability that's really fucking scary and I think it might have something to do with the next movie.

!!!NOW ALL ASS-KICKING UNTIL THE END!!!

ASS-KICKING #1: Neo fights those Blues Brothers–looking dudes and it's pretty fucking cool. But it's just a teaser, like when they have pictures of the food at Jack in the Box, and the tacos look all good in the picture, but then you get some and they look like they got pooped out of a pig. But you eat 'em because there's fries coming. In this movie there's ALWAYS fries coming. **6.**

HEADS UP: There's a lot of boring stuff between Ass-Kicking 1 and 2. There's a sermon by the dude who was in OMEGA MAN, and this underground dance thing that looks like if Pottery Barn had a rave on the Planet of the Gay Apes—but the rave thing is where Neo and Memento Babe "do it." I am bringing my headphones when I see this again on the 15th.

ASS-KICKING #2: Neo and a Kung Fu Phooey go at it in a picnic restaurant. They kick over a big thing of chopsticks, which is kind of cool, and Kung Fu Phooey wears these cool little sunglasses, but that's it. 5. And then Neo and Cookie Lady talk. Then chiggity-check your rectum 'cuz here comes:

ASS-KICKING #2: This fight on a playground where like a hundred Smith Dudes are whomping on Neo like a fat girl eating Fiddle Faddle—it's that intense. Holy shit. The thing goes on for like five minutes and just when you're thinking, "Fuck you Star Wars George" it goes on for another five minutes and then Neo flies away like that Greatest American Hero dude. 10.

ASS-KICKING #3: Neo, Murphus and Memento Babe go to a French restaurant in the Matrix and there's this French dick and you're thinking, "Fuck you for not supporting us against Egypt," and then Neo goes whomp-ass happy on the dude's cohorts while Murphus and Trinity free this Key Dude and fight these Edgar Winter guys with dreadlocks who can turn into ghosts. 8.

ASS-KICKING #4–28: That's right, this next scene feels like 24 ass-kickings. Seriously, the rest of the summer is going to suck busboy cock for ketchup packets compared to this scene.

**HERE'S WHERE I WISH THE ENGLISH LANGUAGE ONLY HAD
THE WORDS "HOLY" "FUCKING" AND "SHIT"**

HOLY

Murphus and Memento Babe have to escape on a huge freeway
(which is a no-no in the Matrix; "It's suicide!" says Memento
Babe, or something like that I can't remember for sure) while the
Ghost Guys chase them, plus the Smiths, who keep taking over
the drivers on the freeway and they're shooting and everything's
blowing up for miles and

FUCKING

**Memento Babe has to go against the traffic on a
fucking motorcycle and they keep trying to smash
her and Murphus takes out the Ghost Guys in this
totally cool way and the fucking samurai sword and
the head-on crash and**

!!!SHIT!!!

**the fucking Blues Brothers guys and razors and
swordfight on top of a truck and Memento Babe
flying through the air and out of nowhere Neo and
I am out!!of!!cum!! 10 10 10 10 10 10 10 10 10 10 10
10 10 10 10 10 10 10 10 10 10 10 10 10 10 10 10 10**

And there's a whole other ass-kicking after this, which I can barely remember because, seriously, that fucking chase scene. It's now #2 on my list of all-time chases, ahead of ARK RAIDERS, where Blade Runner gets dragged behind the Nazi truck (#5), and then DYING IN LOS ANGELES, where CSI is driving the car against the traffic (#4) and then TAXI RONIN, where Taxi Driver guy goes the wrong way down that French tunnel, and also because they keep running over French people (#3), and now MATRIX, right behind BANDIT AND THE FAT GAY GUY 2, where all the police cars and all the trucks play chicken out in the desert (#1).

Neo needs to fight Blade and that fat bald guy from STIR CRAZY.

Then Murphus and Neo and Memento Babe try to raid some sort of central something, like the CPU in TRON, something like that. Smith Dude re-appears, Neo has a talk with a new character, someone dies and someone's reborn. Then something gets destroyed (good), something else gets destroyed (bad), and Neo discovers a new power. Then something BIG gets destroyed (really really bad), and someone lives who shouldn't.

MY HINT: Stay through the credits and you get to see a trailer for **MATRIX: YOU WILL SHIT**, the third movie.

That's it. Best movie of the year. I still want to see HULK-MAN and the werewolf thing and I think there's something where you get to see a hot Asian's boobs, but they're not going to get close to this one. Here's my blurb if they're putting blurbs in ads:

"MATRIX: KINGDOM OF ASS-KICKING is like if all of Anthrax's albums formed into a hot chick who had to fuck you ten times a day or she gets pee-cancer."

Neill Cumpston
5/1/03

The Passion of the "Christ" and Dawning
of the Dead

I just got back from seeing the new zombie movie at midnight at
the Arclight in Hollywood. I got there way early, like three hours,
and I had nothing to do, and I was getting drunk with my friends
at this bar in the lobby. The Arclight looks like MINORITY REPORT
and there's a bar where you can drink, which other theaters should
have if you have to see a movie with Julia Roberts or Ben Affleck
or Freddie Prinze or Steve Martin. Actually, there should be a lot of
actors where if they're in a movie you get a can of beer automatic.
Also certain plots, like if there's a gay friend or a lady ghost.

So we still have all this time, and my one friend says, "We should
see the Jesus movie. I hear it's non-stop ass-kicking." And I like
the sound of that, and I thought for a second that maybe this
was another Jesus movie by the TAXI DRIVER guy, only now he's
put guns and bullets going into heads instead of crying and that
PLATOON guy's dick-hose.

I'll make the Jesus review quick—it fucking rules. It made me
yell, "Jesus Christ on a cross!" even the scenes that *didn't* have
Jesus Christ on a cross. This one's directed by Mel Gibson and he
obviously learned some shit from LETHAL WEAPON 2 because he
gets right to the action. There's a shot of the moon and then right
away there's gladiator dudes beating the crap out of a bunch of
hippies. Jesus is this guy with a super-powered left hand—it's like

he can give people Wolverine powers by touching them with his left hand. He makes a guy's ear grow back but before you know it the gladiator dudes arrest him and beat the be-jeezus out of Jesus for two straight hours. Then they nail him to a cross, and he dies, but not after bleeding enough blood to fill up everyone in CADDYSHACK plus that fat vampire dude in the first BLADE movie. Everyone's pissed at Jesus. They all want him dead. But this is back in Bible times, when they didn't have shotguns and chainsaws, and back then when you want to kill a superhero you have to rain two hours of whomp-ass on him and then nail him to something, sort of like a message to other superheroes. And they must have gotten the message, because there weren't any more superheroes until Superman.

This is a great movie to take a chick to 'cuz it's super-violent but you can sit there like, hey, this doesn't effect me, and she'll think you're a total bad-ass. Then here comes the blowjob. Thank you, Jesus.

The only thing wrong with the movie is why didn't anyone cut off his super-powered left hand, and then use it on other people? Like, you could have a bad guy like in ENTER THE DRAGON, where he puts on different hands—claw hand, flamethrower hand, etc. And one of the hands could be the Jesus hand, and you could heal all your henchmen, or maybe touch yourself while you're kung-fuing someone, so no matter what they do, you can heal.

Also, I like the Satan chick walking around with the baby that has the "Black Hole Sun" face.

The last shot of THE PASSION OF THE "CHRIST" is of Jesus getting up from the dead and walking out of his grave. This is the perfect movie to see right before DAWNING OF THE DEAD because it's like Jesus was the original zombie (O.Z.—only super good-looking and not smelly), so when DAWNING opens it's like it's a sequel. Now it's thousands of years later and the being-a-zombie thing that Jesus started has caught on. In fact, Jesus in the first movie is always telling his buddies to eat his skin and drink his blood. So now it's today, and the zombie followers are taking that idea really fucking seriously.

DAWNING OF THE DEAD rules as hard as THE PASSION, but it so pusses out on the violence. THE PASSION is like, "Hold on, 'cuz I'm going to . . ." and you're waiting for it to say, "Punch you in the balls" but it goes ahead and kicks you in the head and then throws a wrench at your ass until you shit. Still, DAWNING doesn't have the holy-motion John Woo scenes that the PASSION does, so I guess they balance out.

The first ten minutes of DAWNING are big-ass apocalypse, and then credits, and then right back to the apocalypse. A bunch of people who don't get the zombie-bite hide in a shopping mall but here come the zombies so it's shooting and punching and explosions. They don't show zombies sitting down and just eating people, which sucks, but there's a great scene with a zombie baby. If you're trying to convince your dumb-ass girlfriend not to have a baby, this is the movie to take her to. In fact, both PASSION and DAWNING have fucked-up babies, so keep these in mind if you want to win a baby argument.

DAWNING is also a remake of a 70's film, also about zombies. They do a great job of updating it because this movie is set today, rather than the 70's. There's also a cool scene where people on the roof of the shopping mall shoot zombies they think look like celebrities. I think this all the time when I see real celebrities, so it was good for a movie to back me up.

Fuck, I don't know what else to tell you. PASSION and DAWNING is the greatest double-feature ever, but leave enough time in between for that thank-you Jesus blowjob. Eight stars (four for each), and here's an idea for the third movie in the trilogy: Zombie Jesus vs. Freddy vs. Jason vs. That Slinky-Spine Girl from *Pet Semetary*.

Neill Cumpston
3:21 a.m.

Spider Man Part Three

As I said in my electronic e-mail to "Moriarty" (a code name! I hope I don't go to "spy prison"!) Neill got bad poops after having fish tacos at Rubio's (I always get the Southwestern Chicken Salad without the tortilla chips 'cuz "chips go to the hips"—ha ha!) and couldn't attend the screening of Spider-Man Part 3 at the IMAX theater at The Bridge. So he asked if I would go, and turn in this review for him.

I wasn't anxious about missing American Idol tonight (I'm a die-hard "Blake Lady"!) but Neill promised he'd videotape it and, since he's ensconced securely on the living room couch (Mr. Pilkington, my stuffed giraffe, wasn't too happy about being relegated to the ottoman, I can tell you that!) he also said he'd "pause out" the commercials. Trade off accepted, Neill Mampleford Cumpston (he hates when I use his middle name)!

Well, let me be the first (apparently, being "first" is a big deal on this internet web dealie-do) to tell you that Spider Man Part Three is one of the best movies I've ever seen! And I've seen my share, everything from Funny About Love *to* Parenthood! *And this Spider-fellow's got them beat!*

One of my favorite shows is One Tree Hill *(call me young at heart!). Well, this new movie is like three episodes of* One Tree

Hill *put together! Unlike those first Spider-Man movies (which would sometimes play on TV at the senior center right before our Movement to Music class) this one isn't full of yelling and punching and running fast.*

In this one, the director finally focuses on the kinds of things I think Spider-Man fans have been aching for . . . namely, love and forgiveness! (Coincidentally, the names of my belated tabbys!) There's only about twenty-five minutes of actual Spidey footage in this movie—which makes all kinds of room for:

That darling Mary Jane singing (two songs!)

Peter Parker crying

Harry Osborn crying

Harry Osborn hearing Willem Dafoe's voice through a huge painting of Willem Dafoe, and then getting yelled at by Willem Dafoe

This old servant of Harry's suddenly walking into the frame during the third act and explaining a lot of stuff that frankly I was confused about—it didn't even bother me that I didn't know who the old servant was—I love it when old people explain things slowly and carefully in movies

Harry Osborn and Mary Jane cooking an omelet and dancing to Chubby Checker's "The Twist" (my favorite part)

The Sandman crying

Eddie Brock crying

Mary Jane crying

Aunt May crying

Bruce Campbell, from the Evil Dead films, doing a hilarious French accent! The scene goes on for nine minutes, but you could tell the audience wanted it to go on sooooooo much longer, the way they sighed heavily and rolled their eyes when it was over! It's not as funny as the French accent my late husband, Niles, used to do at charade nights, but it came pretty darn close!

Peter Parker doing a sly "revenge jazz dance" in front of Mary Jane when she's trying to sing at one of those modern jazz clubs that Spider-Man fans love so much. This scene also ended way too soon, to make room for some fighting.

And yes, I might as well tell you, there ARE a few action scenes that get in the way of all the interesting stuff between the characters and their relationships and their ordinary, everyday lives.

First, there's a fight between Peter Parker and Harry Osborn (he's something called the New Goblin, and he rides one of those fun-looking skateboards like in the Back to the Future sequels) that kicks off the movie. It's far and away the most exciting sequence in the movie (the audience applauded!) and Peter doesn't even put that silly Spider-man costume on, so we get to see his wonderful facial expressions and mouth-acting.

There's also a new villain played by the wonderful Thomas Haden Church—The Sandman. He's a shape-shifting baddie whose daughter is dying so, even though he gets put through some pretty crazy action sequences, there's plenty of opportunities for him to look sad and cry about things. I wish they'd worked in a line where he's crying, and says, "I've got sand in my eye." Maybe on the DVD.

What's smart about putting the Spider-man/New Goblin sequence first is that none of the other action sequences are as exciting, so you can relax and enjoy Peter and Mary Jane's kooky, mixed-up relationship! There's a lot of wonderful scenes of them misunderstanding each other, and not explaining one obvious and simple thing, which would clear up their problems (and, let's face it, make a pretty boring movie)! There's at least six scenes of them calling each other on the telephone, and one of them almost picking up, or just listening to answering machine messages, and misunderstanding those. I was on the edge of my seat!

Of course, you have to sit through a few more dreadful "action" sequences, but luckily they don't go on very long and, even better, rarely involve people you care about. They introduce this new girl, Gwen Stacy, who's a model or something. There's one scene that starts off promising—a comedy scene where she's doing a modeling job for a copying machine (I mean, the very idea! I was cracking up!) and the photographer is, shall we say, a little "fruity." Well, all of this great comedy gets ruined when an out-of-control crane starts smashing up the building, and she falls out, and Spider-man swings by and saves her. But she's only in a few more scenes, and ends up having almost nothing to do with the plot. I wanted to see more of that kooky photographer!

Peter's Aunt May also gets a lot more screen time in this installment, and she's always giving heartfelt advice. It's good to see a superhero movie finally giving some consideration to us "silver tops"!

In fact, I wish they'd consulted this "silver top" about the Venom character. He's like an evil, gooey Spider-man, but it didn't work for me.

Which was too bad, since the Venom plot is introduced so brilliantly—Peter and Mary Jane are necking in the woods, and the gooey Venom stuff falls out of the sky, unexplained, next to them.

But it gets better—it turns out, Venom is some sort of alien goo that attaches itself to you and makes you super-powerful, and also kind of evil. Our niece, Orudis, used to swallow these charcoal tablets to help her digest food. But it turned out later she was also eating her hair, and at Harriet's cookie exchange party she coughed up this huge gob of hair and charcoal and that's what the Venom stuff looks like in the movie. I wonder if, when the Venom stuff attaches itself to you, it makes you draw penises that look like knives the way Orudis did.

Although, in this movie, the Venom substance makes Peter evil, which you can tell because he gets one of those "emo" haircuts and a black suit—not just his Spidey suit, which turns black, but one of those suits you always see Paris Hilton's boyfriends wearing. And he walks down the street like a black person, and winks at girls a lot. It was like Hannibal Lecter or that Simon Cowell fellow, who should have been nicer to Haley because she was a Christian.

I should warn you—the ending is another one of those dreary, hard-on-the-eyes-and-ears battle royals, with Sandman and the gooey black Spider-man (not Peter anymore, but this character named Eddie Brock) battling Spider-man at a construction site. Luckily, it ends the way a good action sequence should end—with one major character dying, and four other characters standing around, crying and apologizing for everything that's happened. I'm not kidding—I was so touched, and I can't wait for all the Spidey-fans to experience this beautiful, slowly-paced sequence for themselves. Bring your Spidey-hankies!

Also, I was very glad to see the whole plotline about the Sandman and his dying daughter was ignored at the end, as if it never happened. Summertime is for happy stories! A dying little girl belongs in an Oscar movie, am I right?

So, to sum up my review, I didn't think I'd like this movie as much as I did. It will certainly give Georgia Rule *and* License to Wed *a run for their money!*

Thanks Props Kudos

Well, yeah, Mom and Dad. You loved books and you made me love books and there are few better gifts.

The teachers who stood out—Mrs. Lincicome and Mr. Shaver and Mr. Wright and Mr. Richards (still!).

The writers who taught me, through their work, to take care of the word—Willa Cather and Joseph Conrad and Wallace Stevens and Jim Goad and Garret Keizer and most of all Harlan Ellison, who, as of this writing, dwells in the Lost Aztec Temple of Mars, high above the San Fernando Valley, a twisty nautilus shell of a house full of books and Ritz crackers and Jack Kirby's fountain pen. I can't believe Harlan's been my friend, even for these few short years. It started with you in the seventh grade, like it probably did with a lot of people.

Everyone at Scribner—especially copyeditor Aja Pollock, who knew the correct spelling of "Yog-Sothoth."

All my friends, every day and ongoing. I hang out with comedians—the best version of life you can live.

Credits

Graphic story on pp. 71–78 by Matthew Bernier

Illustrations on pp. 106, 108, 110, 112, 114, 116–118 courtesy of Onsmith

Illustrations on pp. 170, 172–173 courtesy of David Lasky

LIFE AND HOW TO LIVE IT (p. 17)

GREEN GROW THE RUSHES (p. 18)

WENDELL GEE (p. 20)

By MIKE MILLS, WILLIAM T. BERRY, PETER LAWR

© 1985 NIGHT GARDEN MUSIC

All Rights on Behalf of NIGHT GARDEN MUSIC Administered by WARNER-TAMERLANE PUBLISHING CORP.

All Rights Reserved

Used by Permission of ALFRED MUSIC PUBLISHING CO., INC.

ABOUT THE TYPE

The text of this book has been set in MT Pugmire Gothic. MT Pugmire is a nonflorid, pre-post-Brutalist "curl-type" vowel recessive, first used in the publication of Giselle Tanhauser's memoir, *The Inkling Group and the Things They Put Inside of Me, Volume 2: Face Holes*.

MT Pugmire Gothic is a trademark of MarkoCorp, Feedlot Ltd., and/or its subsidiaries.

Printed and bound by Voluntary Convict Labor Press, Men's Correctional Facility, Galax, Virginia.